A PHILADELPHIA CHRISTIAN IN BEELZEBUB'S COURT

A STUDY OF THE DIFFERENCES BETWEEN THE EPHESUS/LAODICEA CHURCHES AND THE SMYRNA/PHILADELPHIA CHURCHES

S. C. CUNDIFF

ISBN 978-1-0980-9424-9 (paperback)
ISBN 978-1-0980-9425-6 (digital)

Christian Faith Publishing, Inc.
832 Park Avenue
Meadville, PA 16335
www.christianfaithpublishing.com

Printed in the United States of America

Contents

Preface

A couple of years following my graduation from high school, my wife and I, having been enrolled in education classes at college, had an instructor who recommended his students return to visit the high school which they graduated from or at least a local high school. We decided to visit the school we graduated from in order to observe some of the methodology and student culture which might affect us if we chose to major in secondary education. We were fortunate enough to observe two of the classes in which subjects we had been students, and these classes still had the same teachers presiding.

It turned out to be quite an eye-opener for us. The school administration had changed, and an atmosphere came with the new principal that we would not have thought possible in such a short period of time. When we had attended this school, there was a dress code and a policy of monitoring students' behavior in the hallways. The same teachers taught the same classes in the same style, but the behavior we saw in the hallways caused us to think and to say to each other, "Look what they've done to our school, Hon. Look what they've done to our school." The impression was one of great disapproval and disappointment.

Now, after more than thirty years of evangelical ministry, I think about that line more and more. "Look what they've done to my church, Hon. Look what they've done to my church." I want to make it clear from the very start that I still believe the Christian church is Christ's church! He is the founder and head of the church in heaven and on earth. It is not "my" church. Jesus said, "And I say also unto thee, That thou art Peter, and upon this rock I will build my church; and the gates of hell shall not prevail against it" (Matt. 16:18); and we read, "Salute one another with a holy kiss. The churches of Christ salute you" (Rom. 16:16). Paul the apostle wrote, "And hath put all things under His feet, and gave Him to be the head over all things to the church, which is His body, the fullness of Him that filleth all in all" (Eph. 1:22–23).

I have studied the writings of John Bunyan, Jonathan Edwards, Charles G. Finney, Charles Spurgeon, Oswald Chambers, A. W. Tozer, and more current theologians, such as David Wilkerson; and they all confirm that there is consistency in the truth of the Bible, which I wish to live by. I do not read testimonials for doctrine. I avoid fads and faddish Christianity, which seem to twist the truth while sounding authoritative and sincere. Fads may enhance their authors' purpose of entertaining the goats (as Spurgeon wrote) and enhance their bank accounts; but they do not stand the test of time as the church fathers' writings do, in which it is repeated and urged that the shepherds must be about the feeding of the sheep instead of "clowning" to entertain the goats. It is my belief that the truth of the deity of Jesus the Christ is easily understood when one reads and studies all of the above-mentioned Bible teachers in addition to the Bible itself, the Word of truth.

In July of 1971, when I was born again, converted, and began my life-long acts of repentance, I became part of "the church," the family, the bride of Christ. I now say with praise and humility "my church." When I say "my team" as a member of a football team, I am not making the claim that I own the team but that I am pleased and proud to be a player or even a fan. When I speak of my church, I want to be pleased and proud of being a player and a fan. The purpose for the writing of this book is to help those in the Christian faith not to become deceived as prophesied in 1 Timothy 4:1, "Now the Spirit speaketh expressly that in the latter times some shall depart from the faith, giving heed to seducing spirits, and doctrines of devils."

A few years ago, my wife and I were on vacation from the church where I had been called Pastor/Teacher. We agreed to spend some time visiting churches; we were fact finding and checking the spiritual temperature of the body of Christ. I will not elaborate except to say that we were dismayed to encounter overwhelmingly loquacious pastors, false teachers, inaccurate Bible interpreters, ticklers of ears, and fleshly entertainers. At one church, the pastor announced, "It's time to take our smoke break. Come in when you hear the worship team begin to play," as if it could possibly *be* a worship team. A team of worshippers does not need any smoke break. God's truth has been stolen from the saints by hirelings (John 10:12–13). I pray we true believers will all be able to reflect the true Christ and not a poor imitation of Him.

All scriptures used in this book will be quoted from the *King James Version* of the Holy Bible.

1
Truth or Consequence

Since I first read in the Bible, in the Gospel of John, that "the truth shall make you free," I have been an advocate of basing all my sermons on the positive and negative effects of truth. The truths I write or speak about will be Bible based, not just based on my opinion. The consequence of not telling the truth, not hearing the truth, and/or not putting oneself in a position to learn the truth will always result in bondage to us instead of freedom. With this in mind, I would like to begin with some foundational scriptures. If we deviate from these foundations or twist them, the hellish grip of bondage will become evident in the life of the believer.

In 2 Timothy 3:16, we find, "All scripture is given by inspiration of God, and is profitable for doctrine, for reproof, for correction, for instruction in righteousness." The logical question is why? The answer is found in the next verse: "That the man of God may be perfect, thoroughly furnished unto all good works." Part A of verse 16 has been used by hirelings as well as by true shepherds, but when part B of the verse is taught and experienced, the believer will have the opportunity to acquire the tools necessary for serving the Lord in good works. This part of the verse is not taught by hirelings because they are influenced by their own lack of motivation or by the enemy of God, Satan, who strives to prohibit believers from acquiring and preserving a strong spiritual foundation.

His name is *Satanos* in Greek, which means "adversary" or "enemy." He is also known as the devil, which means "the malignant, evil foe"; and by another Greek word, *Diabulos*, meaning "the one

9

who slanders." Jesus called him the father of lies when He addressed the Jews who wanted to stone Him. Why? Because Jesus knew they were acting on a lie they had believed, and He exposed the truth about this enemy. He told them,

> Ye are of your father the devil, and the lusts of your father ye will do. He was a murderer from the beginning, and abode not in the truth, because there is no truth in him. When he speaketh a lie, he speaketh of his own: for he is a liar and the father of it. (John 8:44)

Let's take a look at our foundational truth verse, 2 Timothy 3:16. Focus on the word *all*. *All* in English, Greek, French, or any of the Oriental languages means *all*. There is no hidden meaning to this word! All what? All scripture. The Old and New Testament verses in *all* sixty-six books of the Bible are inspired of God. When I say God, I mean the Father of Jesus Christ, the Creator, the God of Israel who is known by many other names, including Elohim, El Elyon, and Yahweh. Theologically speaking, He is a nonmaterial personal being, self-existent, self-conscious, and self-determining. He is the One and Only about whom Jesus said, "I and my Father are one" (John 10:30). Let's expound on why all scripture in the Bible has such relevance and importance regarding truth.

Revelation 19:10 says, "…for the testimony of Jesus is the spirit of prophecy." Focus on the word *testimony*. In Greek, it is *marturia*, and from this is derived the English word *martyr*—"a witness who is willing to die for what he believes." This verse is the essence of every genuine prophecy, which is the testimony of Jesus. The Old Testament exists to reveal Christ. Prophets were directed by God to make public declaration (a spoken or written forth telling) or a foretelling (a spoken or written word about future events, many of which are still unfulfilled). Luke 24:27 says, "And beginning at Moses and all the prophets, He expounded unto them in all the scriptures the things concerning Himself." It is also said in John 5:39, where Jesus is speaking to the Jews, "Search the scriptures; for in them ye think ye have eternal life: and they are they which testify of me." Then there is 1 Peter 1:10–11, which says,

> Of which salvation the prophets have enquired and searched diligently, who prophesied of the grace that should come unto you: Searching what, or what manner of time the Spirit of Christ which was in them did signify, when it testified beforehand the sufferings of Christ, and the glory that should follow.

In like manner, the New Testament is inspired by the Holy Spirit for the same purpose. In John 14:26, Jesus reminds the apostles, "But the Comforter, which is the Holy Ghost, whom the Father will send in my name, he shall teach you all things, and bring all things to your remembrance, whatsoever I have said unto you." And in John 16:13–15, He continues,

> Howbeit, when He, the Spirit of truth, is come, He will guide you into all truth: for He shall not speak of Himself; but whatsoever He shall hear, that shall He speak: and He will shew you things to come. He shall glorify Me: for He shall receive of mine and shall shew it unto you. All things that the Father hath are mine: therefore said I, that He shall take of mine and shall shew it unto you.

Speaking to Philip, He said, "…He that hath seen Me hath seen the Father…" (John 14:9). Jesus spoke these words to state plainly that He, himself, is God. Jesus is God. The scriptures are given by God. And for what purpose? According to 2 Timothy 3:16, they are very beneficial to the people of His Kingdom, the saints, who are now joint heirs with Jesus! Wow!

> And if children, then heirs; heirs of God,
> and joint-heirs with Christ; if so be that we suffer
> with Him, that we may be also glorified together.
> (Rom. 8:17)

But stop! We must look closely at the rest of this verse. Too many hirelings forget to point out the prerequisites for many of the more than 5,000 promises in the Bible. The next word is *if*. If? Yes! *If* means maybe so or maybe not. It means there is a matter of choice involved. The verse says, "…if so be that we suffer with Him, that we may be also glorified together." Does that mean that I have to be treated the same way Jesus was treated at Calvary? Maybe. Probably not. But many saints have been crucified or decapitated. The scriptures often indicate that God leads His children through suffering before they reach His glory! Just read the story of Joseph in Genesis or the missionary trips of Paul in the book of Acts.

Our text in 2 Timothy 3:16 says scripture is "profitable for doctrine." So we must ask this question: how does it become profitable? The answer is found in the phrase "given by inspiration of God." This phrase is the best translation of the Greek word *theópneustas*, which means "God-breathed." Why is that important? This tells us that scripture is not the product of man but the product of the direct utterance of God, and that is why we call it the Holy Bible. That is also why we sometimes refer to it as the Word of God. The problem today is that many hirelings have lost their first love, Jesus; and therefore they have lost respect for His Word. They seem to have forgotten that Jesus said, "Heaven and earth shall pass away, but My words shall not pass away" (Matt. 24:35). This brings us to a problem.

> For My thoughts are not your thoughts, nei-
> ther are your ways My ways, saith the Lord. For
> as the heavens are higher than the earth, so are
> My ways higher than your ways and My thoughts
> than your thoughts. (Isa. 55:8–9)

The audience is not just the prophet but the whole human race. Let us add to this conundrum Proverbs 3:5–7:

> Trust in the Lord with *all* [there is that word *all* again] thine heart; and lean not unto thine own understanding. In *all* thy ways acknowledge Him, and He shall direct thy paths. Be *not* wise in thine own eyes: fear the Lord, and *depart* from evil. (emphasis mine)

The word *ways* in verse 6 is the Hebrew word *derek*—it means "a mode of receiving recurring actions." We must, as children of God, stop thinking the old "unsaved" thoughts that lead to unsaved beliefs, resulting in negative attention drawn to ourselves. The next word we need to look at in that verse is *acknowledge*. The Hebrew word is *yada*. This is very important and means "to make direct and intimate contact". The great I AM allows this intimacy with Himself. Do not disregard such an opportunity as this.

The thief and father of lies will try to influence believers to use their own sinful thinking in an attempt to make them insert incorrect thoughts and ways into their understanding of God. It is their own old nature and worldly thinking which sounds authoritative. Something said sincerely may still be in error because it is not God's way. Leaning on your own understanding will cause you to reap consequences instead of reaping truths that will set you free and keep you free.

The promise that God gives to His children in Proverbs 3:6 is a gold mine: "He shall direct thy paths." We can live in such a way that we will not be directed by Satan, not be directed by ourselves, not be directed by any other person who has fallen short of the glory of God—but directed by God Himself. Look at the Hebrew word translated "direct." It is *yashar*. It means to make something straight and correct; it is what God calls uprightness. The question then is whether we wish to have Satan (who will ultimately be thrown into the lake of fire) and the demons or the people of earth (most of whom are not born again) directing our paths, or do we prefer to be directed by the only One who is omniscient? God knows everything about everybody and everything that has ever been or shall ever be. This word is an attribute given only to God, the God of the Bible. He is eternal, and therefore, He eternally knows all things. He is without sin, and therefore, He is perfect and perfectly knows all things which can be known—past, present, and future. He never needs advice or counsel. He knows the correct way to complete His desired work in us.

Do the scriptures tell us about the omniscience of God, or is this just another of those theological words used by theologians? To explore that great question, we will look at the scriptures and the writings of previously mentioned men, who have proven by their fruits to be non-hirelings and have, therefore, been an encouragement to me and many others in the renewing of our minds. Proverbs 15:11 states, "Hell and destruction are before the Lord: how much more then the hearts of the children of men?" If the repugnance of the unseen world is plain to God, then He easily sees also the concealed thoughts of men. The Psalmist says, "He telleth the number of the stars; He calleth them all by their names" (Ps. 147:4). He goes on in the next verse to say, "Great is our Lord, and of great power: His understanding is infinite." The prophet Isaiah wrote, "Declaring the end from the beginning and from ancient times the things that are not yet done, saying, My counsel shall stand, and I will do all my pleasure" (Isa. 46:10).

In the New Testament, we are told that the very hairs of our head are all numbered (Matt. 10:30). Why, then, would I want to lean on my own understanding about any subject in the kingdom of God when I can have the intimate counsel of God instead? The revealed truth of the Word of God does not change with geographical location or generational connotation. Nevertheless, we see this phrase in the Bible: "But God." In His mercy and love, God gives revelation and illumination to those who have asked for it. James 1:5 says, "If any of you lack wisdom, let him ask of God, that giveth to all men liberally, and upbraided not; and it shall be given him." But there is one more warning that I must address. It is found in

Proverbs: "There is a way which seemeth right unto a man, but the end thereof are the ways of death" (Prov. 14:12).

If you are thinking of applying *your* ways to the truth of our text in 2 Timothy 3:16, it will have grave consequences and leave you in bondage. Therefore, let us look again at 2 Timothy 3:16. The God-breathed scripture is profitable, not only for doctrine but for reproof, for correction, and for instruction in righteousness. Let me state right here and now that if you do not like change, then you will not like being a Christian. Christianity is all about change! The way of man consists of being born while the way of God consists of being born *again*. The way of man means to think there is nothing wrong with you, but the way of God is to be convicted of sin and repent. The way of man means you should be a tough guy, but the way of God means to surrender meekly and be teachable. Christians yield and think of others instead of always thinking of themselves. They ask for help from the Holy Spirit as well as from those God has delegated as His "spokespersons," and they recognize that they need to renew their minds in order to think more like God. They find correct instruction in Romans 12:2, which says, "And be not conformed to this world; but be ye transformed by the renewing of your mind, that ye may prove what is that good, and acceptable, and perfect will of God." Some might protest that this sounds legalistic. No! It is Bible-istic!

"I do not need reproof or correction," some might proudly state. What they really mean is that they do not want the interpretation or correction from the pastor because they are "so loved by God." They have forgotten that you and I were mightily loved by God before Adam was created.

> The Lord hath appeared of old unto me,
> saying, Yea, I have loved thee with an everlasting
> love: therefore with loving kindness have I drawn
> thee. (Jer. 31:3)

Since God has no beginning or end and John tells us that God is love, He has *always* loved, and He cannot stop! Love does not mean never correcting, though. We like to call it "tough love" in our vernacular, but the writer of Hebrews quotes these verses from Proverbs, saying, "My son, despise not thou the chastening of the Lord, nor faint when thou are rebuked of Him: For whom the Lord loveth He chasteneth, and scourgeth every son whom He receiveth" (Heb. 12:5–6). The word *chastening* in Hebrew means "discipline." God says I need chastening and discipline, so I gladly pray to be convicted by the Holy Spirit concerning my need for direct or delegated rebuke and correction. It proves that I am loved by the great I AM! But the hirelings have removed, without approval from God, the teachings regarding this kingdom-of-God truth. This has consequences and no overcoming victories.

All saints suffer, but many times, we use the word *suffering* to describe reaping what we have sown ourselves. This is not a chastening of the Lord, nor does it mean that God is unconcerned about our well-being. Through the experiences of discipline, God reveals Himself to be a true Father. Chastening describes ongoing corrective discipline, which all good fathers—especially God the Father—employ in training their children. It is never administered in a crude, rigorous, or unfeeling way but always in love, with the molding hand of a tenderhearted Savior who never stops thinking about His child. He thus brings us to spiritual maturity.

He allows this ongoing process, which does not end as long as we live on earth, so that we will renew our minds and may therefore be transformed to the conformity He deserves: conformed to the image of His only begotten Son, Jesus. It is a lengthy, ongoing process wherein we gain information, which leads to transformation. But the goal is conformation—we must be conformed in every point to the image of Christ. This is the process which takes us from glory to glory (2 Cor. 3:18).

Glory in Hebrew is the word *kabad*; and it means "splendor, honor, and copiousness." Literally it infers the weightiness and visible splendor of the Almighty God. The Greek word for this is *doxa*, referring to dignity and honor. This lets us know why it is such a lengthy process. We cannot gain kingdom-of-God information in sound bites like we gain worldly information. The hirelings pass these sound bites on to their congregations as if they have real information when all they really have is a sprinkling of mixed ideas. What then is His goal, you ask? The answer is found in Ephesians 5:1: "Be ye therefore followers of God as dear children."

The Holy Spirit is not being harsh when He says, "Seek those things which are above" (Col. 3:1). Neither is He being harsh when He says, "Set your affection on things above, not on things on the earth" (Col. 3:1).

> Love not the world, neither the things that
> are in the world. If any man love the world, the
> love of the Father is not in him. (1 John 2:15)

I almost believe some who sit under the false teachings of these hirelings pray that they can take their collections of wood, hay, and stubble with them when Christ returns for His bride.

In the following chapters, I hope to show the truths needed to bring us out of the slavery and bondage brought about by the false teaching of hirelings. The Christians who read their Bibles know John 1:12, John 3:16–17, Acts 2:21, Romans 3:23, Romans 6:23, Romans 10:9–10; and they never forget Ephesians 2:8 and the excessively misused Revelation 3:20. All are truths, but hirelings just change the order around and say it as if the whole congregation has never heard it before. They rarely teach about the armor of God or spiritual warfare. In the entire first five years of my salvation experience (my born-again event), I never heard a single message about quenching the Spirit of God. Nor did I hear any messages about abstaining from the appearance of evil or not despising prophesying, yet all these instructions are found in 1 Thessalonians 5. Hirelings sometimes mention these in passing but do not teach how to live this kind of life. When I accepted Jesus as my Savior, I attended for a time a church which used a hymnbook containing 300 hymns; but the church song leaders persisted in singing their favorite 20 hymns plus a few for Christmas, Easter, and other holidays, over and over. I attended with my wife, and we never missed Sunday school and something they called worship service, which was a meeting that must begin at 11:00AM Sunday morning and be over by 12:00PM. This type of ritual in an evangelical church stunted my spiritual growth. The hireling had reached his own spiritual plateau years before I was saved. "Amazing Grace" was sung habitually and usually with the congregation looking at their watches or telling the children to sit still. This type of spiritual compromise has brought about many consequences.

2
To Do or Not to Do…
That Is the Question

King Saul of Israel gave the church of Jesus Christ an example of being religious but not being serious about His kingdom assignments. He, like many of us, thought about kingdom-of-God concepts with the natural mind; and that always ends up in disaster. When God gives one of His servants an assignment, that person should ask the Assigner for His directions. How? Where? When? And that person should never lean on his or her own understanding even if God has asked him to do something that He has asked many times before. God is, has been, and always will be sovereign.

> For I am the Lord, I change not; therefore
> ye sons of Jacob are not consumed. (Mal. 3:6)

We, the people of God by invitation, grace, mercy, and love, must do the changing if we wish to be in alignment with God—His will, His teachings, and His ways. King Saul never learned this or perhaps forgot it. We read in 1 Samuel that King Saul had been given another military assignment. The battle, as usual, was for the purpose of punishing an enemy of God and Israel. Saul did this, but he departed from his assignment by adding to his role of military leader the ministry of the priesthood. He thought that God would be pleased. We often fall into that thinking, as well, when we think we understand God.

In contrast, Joshua and Caleb did not attempt to interpret God according to their own experience. God said, "But My servant Caleb, because he had another spirit with him, and hath followed Me fully, him will I bring into the land whereinto he went; and his seed shall possess it" (Num. 14:24). We see from verse 20 that God is speaking. These two were more like King David in heart, but King Saul did not have the heart God sought and was disciplined.

> But now thy kingdom shall not continue; the Lord hath sought Him a man after His own heart, and the Lord hath commanded him to be captain over his people, because thou hast not kept that which the Lord commanded thee. (1 Sam. 13:14)

Saul could not repent, receive instruction, or cleave to the commandment of God as David did, as evidenced by the actions and writings of David in the Psalms. Neither did Saul have the leadership qualities that Joshua possessed. A man of God will always be free to choose, and like Joshua, we must be able to make decisions that flow against popular demands and opinions. A shepherd, unlike a hireling, must look at the situation at hand and call the flock to increase their faith in God and His promises, not keep gazing at the impossible temporary circumstances. Real leaders of the people of God do not make decisions based on sentiment, especially if it is temporary change or just a convenient way to table a problem. They never give in to moroseness like Eeyore, the friend of Winnie the Pooh.

Spiritual progress requires faith, and unbelief will never see beyond the difficulties. An example of this is the commissioning of the twelve spies, one from each of the tribes, with Joshua selected as leader. He and Caleb were of a different spirit, and therefore, they did not respond like the other ten spies who could only see giants and could see nothing of the presence and power of the great I AM! In very much the same way, King Saul and his army could only see the battle-hardened Philistine army against them, but the shepherd boy David saw the uncircumcised Philistine blaspheming his God.

The history of Saul shows that he repeatedly thought carnally and made his decisions accordingly. He did the "normal" thing when he decided not to wait for Samuel to officiate at the appointed sacrificial offering because it felt "normal" to him to be in a hurry and take charge when someone seemed to be late. Samuel was not late. Saul did not do the will of God. God had said to wait for Samuel. This brought a life-changing result to Saul and the people of Israel. The response of God was "It repenteth Me that I have set up Saul to be king: for he is turned back from following Me, and hath not performed My commandments. And it grieved Samuel; and he cried unto the Lord all night" (1 Sam. 15:11). Pay close attention to what God says next (to all His people of every generation):

> And Samuel said, Hath the Lord as great delight in burnt offerings and sacrifices, as in obeying the voice of the Lord? Behold, to obey is better than sacrifice, and to hearken than the fat of rams. For rebellion is as the sin of witchcraft, and stubbornness is as iniquity and idolatry. Because thou hast rejected the word of the Lord, He hath also rejected thee from being king. (1 Sam. 15:22–23)

You might ask just what was this horrendous disobedience that King Saul committed? He leaned on his own understanding and thought he was wise in his own eyes just as Adam and Eve did. God had made it very clear to Moses (and Saul knew it well) that only those of the tribe of Levi could be priests. And the priests were the only ones who could make offerings. Saul committed an unrighteous act in officiating at a ceremony for burnt offerings. The offerings were not received by God, who wants and deserves obedience. This sin, like all other sin, caused a separation from God.

Yes, Saul was still loved by God, as all sinners are. And yes, this sin and all our sin may be forgiven when we acknowledge it as sin. It is not just a mistake. It is an *intentional* placing of our filth and rebellion on our pure and holy God. We must feel the burden of each act so that we can repent with godly sorrow instead of worldly sorrow, regretting that we've been caught. Psalm 103:3 says God forgives all our iniquities and heals all our diseases. The word for *forgives* in Hebrew is *salach*, which in the simplest form means "to pardon." But the deeper meaning of this word is "to relieve someone of the burden of their offense." We must feel the burden of our offense before we can feel the relief of having it forgiven.

A wise man once said that there were things he used to do but does not do anymore, not because they are against the rules but because they are against his heart. When we grow to this level, we will feel the burden of each offense. And what are the ramifications for us if we do not obey this directive? Our prayers will be heard but not answered. Does the blood of Christ still make us clean in the eyes of God? Yes, but only because He sees us through the cleansing blood of Christ. And will we lose our salvation? No. How about our blessings? Blessings will not come our way until we confess our sin and repent. And even in our blessings, we will be required to reap what we have sown. If we harden our hearts and avoid the narrow path we are called to walk on, we show that we have now entered into stubbornness, and God sees stubbornness as idol worship.

I have personally witnessed this "King Saul attitude." It runs rampant in the church today. We, like King Saul, cannot afford to keep standing in opposition to the commands of God. They are still commands and not suggestions. I pray that all of us who call ourselves saints of God will pray for revelation truth so that we may have the mind of Christ to give us kingdom understanding; then we will know that to hear the Word of God and not practice it is the same as rejecting it. Jesus said, "And why call ye Me, Lord, Lord, and do not the things which I say?" (Luke 6:46).

Satan wants to place us and keep us in a generic, non-surrendered relationship. The generic relationship is with God in general, but the non-surrendered relationship means we think He is not Lord and He is not in charge. But actually, He *is* the boss. He calls the shots; and we ought to obey out of love, not like robots. Satan wants us to believe we should have a say in the events of our lives. He wants us to forget that we have been purchased, bought with a price (1 Cor.

TO DO OR NOT TO DO… THAT IS THE QUESTION

6:19). Satan and the world want us to forget that the price was the precious blood of Jesus! "For ye are bought with a price: therefore glorify God in your body, and in your spirit, which are God's" (1 Cor. 6:20). Whose are they? God's! Because Christians have been purchased by the blood of Christ, they should honor Him to whom they belong.

The remainder of this book will focus on how to honor Jesus and how to recognize and change what is not honoring to Jesus. However, if the scripture given thus far does not make sense to you or sounds like foolishness to you, I would like to explain why that is happening. We approach from a biblical perspective though not perhaps a denominational perspective or a hireling perspective (John 10:12–13).

The Bible is not a world history book although it covers a lot of history. It is the history of salvation for mankind and the history of God's dealings with His creation. The Old Testament names people of historical notoriety, such as Nebuchadnezzar, the king of the neo-Babylonian empire. The New Testament names Augustus Caesar, Tiberius Caesar, and Claudius Caesar. In addition, the Bible is not a geography book though many geographical references are mentioned, e.g., the Sea of Galilee, Rome, the Tigris River, Egypt, and Jerusalem. All of these are still in the same locations. The scriptures, except for the salvation passages, such as John 3:16 and Romans 10:9–10, cannot be understood or will be extremely difficult to understand until one is born again and becomes a new creature in Christ. If one is born again and not spiritually minded but worldly minded or naturally minded, they cannot receive the things of the Spirit of God. They cannot receive the Bible because the whole Bible came from the Spirit of God.

> For the preaching of the cross is to them
> that perish foolishness; but unto us which are
> saved it is the power of God. (1 Cor. 1:18)

> But the natural man receiveth not the things
> of the Spirit of God: for they are foolishness unto

him: neither can he know them, because they are spiritually discerned. (1 Cor. 2:14)

Most of the churches in America are occupied by carnal Christians and have been for over five decades. The hirelings (called pastors) have not told their congregations the full gospel or the whole truth which will set them free from thinking and living as if they have never believed in Christ. New converts are excluded from this group. Nobody expects a six-month-old child to read or talk or feed himself. The same principle applies to a "babe" in the Lord. Jesus relates lessons from the parable of the fig tree in Luke 13:6–9 and the parable of the sower and the seeds in Matthew 13:3–9. Remember, spiders are found in a church, but that does not mean they are Christians.

This book is for Christians who hate being carnal and wish to be fully alive in His Spirit, but they need some help to find out what they should do. If that is you, stop and ask the Holy Spirit for help. He is the Great Helper and only Comforter you will ever need. If you need to take a companion dog to church instead of the Holy Spirit, you have an idol. The Holy Spirit has given us guidance to help us transfer our desire into ability. These principles apply to any kingdom-of-God teachings.

When you read a scripture or hear a message or perhaps listen to a CD, the Holy Spirit convicts you and places Bible truth into your mind so that you desire that truth for your life. Then what? The desire was put there after you received your new nature in the same manner as the Holy Spirit gave you a desire to seek and know Him before you were saved. He has put within us a desire to please Him. You now will want to do as Jesus did.

> And He that sent Me is with Me: the Father hath not left Me alone; for I do always those things that please Him. (John 8:29)

So now we want to do the things that please God, whom we can now call our Father since we are born again. We previously experienced the first birth by the seed of sinful man, but now are born again of the seed of God. This act of pleasing the Father will free us from all bondage! You may not be as rich as Paul McCartney or Tom Hanks, which was not promised anyway; but you will be free from bondage—and that is truly free. We must learn that the desire to do these things that are pleasing to God the Father is entirely different from having the ability to do the things which please the Father.

The battle now begins. What about all the other strong desires I have that are in conflict with the newly born spiritual desire? What about ideas, opinions, and desires of my parents or spouse or children or grandchildren? We cannot please the Great Jehovah when we are boxed in by the desire to please others or even ourselves. The new nature from God must be in alignment with the unchangeable God. This new nature in us is like the nature of Christ. The new nature is the only source from which my new desire can originate. So how do I go from desire to ability? I can only do it by getting closer to God and His Word, which will begin to renew my old mind to conform to Jesus as my all in all.

Any advance toward proper alignment which comes from the true Word of God initiates the development of a balance between the desire to please God and the ability to perform it. The old problem is my character. Nature is given to me, but my character is developed. Non-biblical role models and earthly teachings sound acceptable, but after we are awakened, we realize that they are not just unacceptable but also disastrous.

As the character of a saint is developed by the Word of God, it is soon obvious that casual Bible reading or hearing slows down the developmental process. There is a lack of concentration and commitment to the truth of the Word of God. But continually receiving His Word puts us "on the freeway" and takes us off the dilapidated, winding, two-lane road. Then as the old character dies and the new character comes alive in developmental stages, our desire to please God grows into the ability to please God. Where does this happen? It happens in the renewed heart of the believer.

When Jesus said, "I always do those things that please My Father," He was referring to the desire of His Father. Our desiring what the Father desires will create one of two conclusions: positive or negative. The positive one will cause your thoughts to rejoice the heart of God by pleasing Him through your actions and reactions. The negative one happened to the Apostle Paul as related in Romans 7:15, "For that which I do I allow not: what I would, that do I not; but what I hate, that do I." And then he says in verse 24, "O wretched man that I am! Who shall deliver me from the body of this death?" The second part of that verse asks a very important question. Who shall deliver me from the body of this death? The answer comes in verse 25:

> I thank God through Jesus Christ our Lord.
> So then with the mind I myself serve the law of
> God; but with the flesh the law of sin.

This is the answer we need. Notice Paul did not say our Savior or our God or our Teacher. Our victory and deliverance comes as we surrender to the Lordship of Christ!

3

It Will Not Be Easy

Becoming a Christian or a member of the bride of Christ, the Church, is easy. Remaining one, however, requires much work! It will take a lot of praying (talking *with* God, not *to* God) and listening to Him more than talking. When two people talk at the same time, it is not conversation; it is only frustrating babble. One person should be listening while the other one is talking—listening, not thinking about a comeback or daydreaming about anything else. Jesus said in John 10 that He, and only He, was the Great Shepherd. He also said this:

> But He that entereth in by the door is the Shepherd of the sheep. To Him the porter openeth; and the sheep hear His voice: and He calleth His own sheep by name, and leadeth them out. And when He putteth forth His own sheep, He goeth before them, and the sheep follow Him: for they know His voice. (John 10:2–4)

In the agriculturally based society of Jesus's time, as well as the high-tech world of today, everyone knew and knows that Jesus was speaking metaphorically. He is the same Good Shepherd that David wrote of in Psalm 23 and we, the converted believers and saints of God, are the sheep. Here is the point: get as close as possible, as often as possible to hear the Lord speak. If not, you will hear other convenient voices: yours, enemy voices, religious voices, and worldly voices—all trying to imitate His voice. Satan will show up as an angel of light (2 Cor. 11:14) or send a demon or influence a hireling to speak religion to you instead of truth, just as he did to Eve in the Garden of Eden (Gen. 3). Our only escape from this snare and bondage is a two-step process. First, surrender yourself to the Lordship and ownership of Jesus Christ.

> That at the name of Jesus every knee should bow, of things in heaven, and things in earth, and things under the earth; and that every tongue should confess that Jesus Christ is Lord, to the glory of God the Father. (Phil. 2:10–11)

The next part is equally important.

> Submit yourselves therefore to God. Resist the devil, and he will flee from you. Draw nigh to God, and He will draw nigh to you. Cleanse your hands, ye sinners; and purify your hearts, ye double minded. (James 4:7–8)

So what needs to be accomplished in order to understand what the desire (will) of God is for us? And how can we have the ability to please Him? After leaving the non-Pentecostal but evangelical denomination which my wife and I had originally attended, we found ourselves agreeing more and more with the biblical teaching we had heard in an Assembly of God church. I remember sitting in the choir when someone in the congregation gave a prophetic word. This happened almost thirty-five years ago and came as a warning and an encouragement. The message, which I have paraphrased, proclaimed that in the near future, there would be an invasion of New Age disruptions in the form of lying spirits, causing doubts in the doctrines of every evangelical denomination. It might come through someone in a Sunday school class or a Bible study, or a choir member might innocently insert questions that sounded sincere but were actually straight from the pit of hell. They would be pretenders who knew the language of the church and could use it to tempt anyone without discernment to question the truth. They would blatantly attack the statements of faith, such as the virgin birth and the resurrection, with cultural concepts and explanations. They would turn Christian morals and ethics into gray areas of doubt. They would promote an easy believe-ism, advocate a discontinuance of altar calls, and encourage new Bible translations because "the King James Version is just too difficult for modern converts to understand."

The liberal-minded and their disciples agree that Jesus came to earth as a common man but without sin. They understand that He ate with sinners, was kind to lepers, associated Himself with tax collectors and harlots; but somehow they skip right up to the subtle question: shouldn't we speak and act like the unsaved and un-churched in order to set the same example as Jesus, which in turn will make humanity more willing to hear the gospel? In their opinion, this is being Christ-like.

And what has happened to 1 Peter 1:14–16? It is not preached or taught.

> As obedient children, not fashioning your-
> selves according to the former lusts in your igno-
> rance: But as He which hath called you is holy, so
> be ye holy in all manner of conversation; Because
> it is written Be ye holy; for I am holy.

The word *conversation* in the King James Bible means very simply, "your lifestyle—speaking, thinking, and living." And conveniently, they do not teach on 1 Timothy 3:15.

> But if I tarry long, that thou mayest know
> how thou oughtest to behave thyself in the house
> of God, which is the church of the living God,
> the pillar and ground of the truth.

Paul is clearly saying that there is a certain way Christians ought to behave themselves in the house of God. Teaching this is not legalistic; it is Bible-istic.

If a person is holy because he is born again, then why did the Holy Spirit instruct Peter to tell the saints to "be holy"? John, in his epistle 1 John 3:2–3, says to the redeemed, "Beloved, now are we the sons of God, and it doth not yet appear what we shall be: but we know that when He shall appear, we shall be like Him; for we shall see Him as He is." Pay close attention to the next verse, and think about whom John (and ultimately, God) might be addressing this word to. John is addressing the "Beloved," but then verse 3 says, "And every man that hath this hope in Him purifieth himself, even as He is pure."

Look at that word: *pure*. The Greek word is *hagnos*, an adjective. It comes from the root *hagiou*, which means "holy." It describes a morally faultless and modest person; a clean person. God sets the standard for moral faultlessness and modesty, and God determines who is a clean person. If the world proclaims that the "new modesty" is untucked shirts, should we follow the standard of the world or of God? If the standard of modest behavior and morals is to wear only bikini swimsuits the size of an eye patch, will the Christian young women do the same? Probably. Remember when only bikers and sailors had tattoos? And what can we expect when major epidemics, as prophesied, engulf the earth? Will the saints continue to avoid church even after the danger is past? The church is supposed to follow Christ, not the world!

Where did all this come from? Hirelings and weak pastors who want to please men and not please God. They approve of lowering the standards and even quote Paul, "To the weak became I as weak, that I might gain the weak; I am made all things to all men, that I might by all means save some" (1 Cor. 9:22). However, the context is found in verse 19, "I made myself servant…" It is all about humbling oneself; it is not about going into the tavern and drinking beer to save beer drinkers, or going to a harlot in order to save harlots, or joining the KKK in order to save a racist bigot.

When I ministered to the prisoners at McNeal Island Federal Prison, I told them the gospel unashamedly. I did not act or look or talk like these prisoners. We have been told to be sanctified. That word means to be set apart to God and for God!

> But sanctify the Lord God in your hearts:
> and be ready always to give an answer to every
> man that asketh you a reason of the hope that is
> in you with meekness and fear." (1 Pet. 3:15)

We have to decide to be set apart for God. This is not easy. It takes surrender, yielding, and dying to self. Jesus sanctified Himself, knowing that it was the will of the Father for Him to do so. He has sanctified His bride, the church, for Himself; however we need to follow His example and obey the words of instruction in 1 Thessalonians 4:4: "That every one of you should know how to possess his vessel (body) in sanctification and honor."

How did this doctrine cease and disappear from Bible schools and churches? It was taught by all of our early spiritual leaders, including Edwards, Booth, Finney, Spurgeon, Whitefield, and David Wilkerson. The answer is that lukewarmness became the norm. And how did it become normal to be lukewarm? The Christians began to agree with the Scriptures, but they did not believe the Scriptures. For example, they agree that the Word became flesh and dwells amongst them; but as soon as a crisis comes along, they no longer believe that He dwells amongst them, and their actions show that they think the problem is bigger than the God who dwells amongst them. Jesus asks a very important question at the conclusion of the parable of the unjust judge in Luke 18:8. He says, "Nevertheless, when the Son of Man cometh, shall He find faith on the earth?" Why is this such an important question? In the original language, this question required a yes or no answer; the answer here is specifically no.

There are two other scriptural examples which illustrate spiritual lukewarmness. The first is found in 1 John 4:4: "because greater is He that is in you, than He that is in the world." The lukewarm Christians agree with the truth that clearly states the greatness of the

One who is in you, i.e., the Holy Spirit; but as soon as a crisis comes up, they really don't believe that the Holy Spirit is greater than the crisis. The second example is in the much beloved and often memorized Psalm 23:4.

> Yea, though I walk through the valley of the shadow of death, I will fear no evil: for Thou art with me; Thy rod and Thy staff they comfort me.

According to this verse, which many have memorized and agree with but have no faith in, who is being referenced in the phrase "Thou art with me"? Verse 1 tells us who it is—the Lord, my Shepherd. Again, many agree with this but do not believe that the Creator of the whole universe is with them. Rather than being on fire and alive for Jesus, the saints become lukewarm, having no fear of the ramifications of being lukewarm.

As Satanic influence invaded the public schools (via Darwinism and Existentialism taught by Kierkegaard, Nietzsche, and Sarte, and the cult of nihilism), this error soon sifted down into even the Bible colleges and seminaries. I personally know this to be true because I graduated from one of them. In fact, this evil anti-God and anti-absolute truth doctrine soon had a stranglehold on humanity that was worse than Simon Legree. One of the first doctrines to be compromised was the one established by God in Ezekiel 22:26.

> Her priests have violated my law, and have profaned mine holy things: they have put no difference between the holy and profane, neither have they shewed difference between the unclean and the clean, and have hid their eyes from my sabbaths and I am profaned among them.

When my wife and I were first saved in 1971, via Campus Crusade for Christ ministry to college students, we had an immediate hunger for the Bible and prayer and would not allow ourselves to miss a Sunday school or church service. Practically every church in that county had Sunday school classes, Sunday morning services, Sunday evening services, and mid-week teaching or prayer meetings. But soon the world opened all kinds of distractions around the churches, and the people of God slowly declined in church attendance. Fun replaced God, TV replaced prayer, and sports became a full-time false god.

The hirelings stopped distinguishing between the clean and the unclean, the holy and the unholy for two reasons (neither of which is from the Holy Spirit): first, they were practicing what they were telling the sheep not to do; and second, the congregations were subjected to erroneous teaching on "judging." The public knew the "church" was doing all the things it had been telling them not to do and called the believers hypocritical; and they were, in fact, quite hypocritical. The church was soon straddling the fence, forgetting that Satan owns the fence. To top this, the hirelings preached or taught only the beginning of 2 Timothy 3:16 regarding the work of the Spirit. They conveniently left out the part that was taught strongly in yesteryear, which says, "Profitable for doctrine, for reproof, for correction, for instruction in righteousness."

We need instruction in righteousness, we need reproof, and we need biblically sound correction. Paul repeats this truth just a few verses later in 2 Timothy 4:2, "reprove, rebuke"; and when instructing Titus, Paul tells him, "This witness is true. Wherefore rebuke them sharply, that they may be sound in the faith" (Titus 1:13). Why such words? Because in 2 Timothy 4:3–4 Paul warns,

> For the time will come when they will not
> endure sound doctrine; but after their own lusts
> shall they heap to themselves teachers, having
> itching ears; and they shall turn away their ears
> from the truth, and shall be turned unto fables.

I have seen this in my time and heard it with my own ears. When a true shepherd presents the whole truth, that pastor will often be told, "You are judging me!" Anyone who answers his pastor this way has forgotten what Jesus said in John 7:24, "Judge not according to the appearance, but judge righteous judgment." That's right. We are commanded to make a decision, an evaluation, a righteous judgment. That is what Paul did as well in 1 Corinthians 5:3, which says, "For I verily, as absent in body, but present in spirit, have judged already, as though I were present, concerning him that hath so done this deed." And in verse 12, he clearly explains the judging issue: "For what have I to do to judge them also that are without? Do not ye judge them that are within?" And then comes the verse that the hirelings of today really do not like—verse 13: "But them that are without, God judgeth. Therefore put away from among yourselves that wicked person."

The church fathers from Christ to George Washington were teaching the truth found in 1 Timothy 3:15.

> But if I tarry long, that thou mayest know
> how thou oughtest to behave thyself in the house
> of God, which is the church of the living God,
> the pillar and ground of the truth.

What this says to me, along with the aforementioned church fathers, is that the church will have shaky pillars and be on shaky ground if we do not continue to teach how to behave in the house of God, the church (the body as well as the building). The biblical standard of what is holy and not holy from Ezekiel 22 and many other scriptures is what the Apostle Paul used to determine how to biblically judge and call this person wicked. So if you do not use righteous judgment, you will never evaluate whether a person is saved or not, and Satan will say to you, "Careful now. Do not judge"; and this will cause you to never pray for someone to become born again or to repent. Soon you will join the liberal group who say, "Jesus died for all, so all are saved." It is an old, old trick of the devil.

4

How Not to Become a Member of the Ephesus Church

The church at Ephesus had Paul, Timothy, and John as its founding fathers and teachers. There is not a pastor today as anointed, equipped, or approved by God as these three. Yet the church at Ephesus, as explained in Revelation chapter 2, received rebuke from Jesus, who is "the Author and Finisher of our faith" (Heb. 12:2). Unfortunately, some modern translations used by hirelings proclaim erroneously that Jesus is the "Pioneer" of our faith. Perhaps they don't know the difference between God who created and creates, and Daniel Boone who explored.

Jesus criticizes them: "Nevertheless I have somewhat against thee, because thou hast left thy first love" (Rev. 2:4). Wow! They have left their love of the only One who purchased their salvation with His sinless blood and was raised from dead as He said He would be and ascended back to heaven to be seated at the right hand of God. This is the One who acts as our Friend, Redeemer, Constant Companion, King of kings, Deliverer, and Supreme Advocate—all without sleep or a day off. Satan, the flesh, and the world must be better thieves and liars than American politicians. Place yourself in a den of Daniels and find out how you won't lose your first love, Jesus, the soon returning Champion!

What are the warning signals that a person or church has lost its first love? A paraphrase which is credited to Charles Spurgeon explains it well: "There will come a time when the shepherds will not feed the sheep, but clowns will entertain the goats." When the sheep of the Good Shepherd hunger for world-like entertainment delivered by comedic speakers and rock-and-roll or rockabilly imitators serving as "worship teams", and the people become so arrogantly stubborn that they refuse the conviction of the Holy Spirit, then God has already called them idol worshippers. Sadly, I have witnessed this very thing.

We briefly attended an independent, non-Pentecostal, evangelical church where a person was engaged as organist, accompanist, and choir director. He could play very well, but we soon noticed that during the sermon, he went out the side door and played basketball with the youth group boys. He finally admitted his homosexuality and later died of AIDS. A few years later, I was the drummer on a worship team which had a great lead guitarist. He had played for a well-known gold-record recording artist. Through the mercy of God, a sex offender poster appeared at the local post office and alerted the church staff to his background. The pastor announced at a staff meeting that our guitar player was a known child molester. Of course, he had to be dismissed, but the church suffered the upheaval of the necessity of fighting the world on church grounds.

These "Ephesus" pastors began leaving their first love, and that led to compromise and laziness. They didn't do their homework. When you have Jesus as your first love, you will do your utmost for His honor, glory, and Kingship. That is what Paul did and instructed his church to do in Philippians 1:20.

> According to my earnest expectation and
> my hope, that in nothing I shall be ashamed,
> but that with all boldness, as always, so now also
> Christ shall be magnified in my body, whether it
> be by life, or by death.

The church at Ephesus left their first love. What does *left* mean? The Greek word used is *aphieml*, which means "to send away, forsake, lay aside, or leave," similar to divorce as we see it today. We see this word used in Matthew 4:11, wherein the devil leaves Jesus after trying to tempt Him. It is translated as "laying aside" in Mark 7:8, where Jesus is rebuking and correcting the hypocritical Pharisees because they "left" the commandment of God but hearkened to the traditions of men. It is translated to the English "went out" in John 4:30, where we see the story of the Samaritan woman. Jesus asked for water and then told the woman that she had had five husbands and was living in sin with a non-husband at the time. When she told her friends about Jesus, they "went out" to see Christ.

The church at Ephesus neglected Christ's love, forsook Christ's love, and was going to leave His love alone. What is *love* then? The Greek word used is *agape*. It is "a demonstrated affection and benevolence." The extreme example is Christ's death at Calvary. We, in turn, through the power of the Holy Spirit, obey (1 John 2:3–6), thus demonstrating agape love. Our demonstration of godly affection for other believers is showing benevolence as Jesus said in John 13:35, "By this shall all men know that ye are My disciples, if ye have love one to another." The tough one is laying down your life for a friend (John 15:13). This type of love comes from God and is not originated from a human source. It can be counterfeited by force, but then it is not really love. This type of love is entirely *voluntary*, and it must be nurtured and brought to life in the believer.

Look at its source: "He that loveth not knoweth not God; for God is love" (1 John 4:8). Look at what God has done for you and for me: "The love of God is shed abroad in our hearts by the Holy Ghost which is given unto us" (Rom. 5:5). This is *agape*, our English word being *love*. It denotes an undefeatable benevolence and unconquerable goodwill that always seeks the highest good of the other person (his salvation)—no matter what that person does or has done. This love is given freely without asking anything back, and it never considers the worth of who it is given to. It differs from *philos*, another Greek word for love, which involves coincidence and personal choice rather than emotion. Agape is the unconditional, no-strings-attached love that Father God has for the human race.

Satan uses all his subtle, almost hypnotic, lies to try to get Christians to think lower thoughts of God and His ways and teachings than is true or deserved. We know this to be true because of what happened to the church at Ephesus with its overwhelming number of backsliders and carnal Christians. Ask yourself, then, when did you last hear a teaching or sermon regarding the fear of God or the consuming fire of God or any topic other than the love, mercy, and grace of God? Satan, the world, and the hirelings have no desire for us to hear a sermon on Matthew 22:37–38, where "Jesus said unto him, thou shalt love the Lord thy God with all thy heart, and with all thy soul, and with all thy mind. This is the first and great commandment."

Jesus tells the church at Ephesus that He knows their works, labors, and patience. We all should be practicing these things but not at the expense of withholding from God the love He deserves. The same happens today in most hireling-led churches. Their priorities are out of alignment. They forget to seek the Giver and not just the gift. Matthew 6:33 has unfortunately been misread by many; and false translations have caused people to seek a kingdom, but they don't say *whose* kingdom. They also proclaim a good life will be added as if you deserve it and have done God a favor by believing in the salvation given by Christ. For the sake of comparison, here is Matthew 6:33 from the KJV:

> But seek ye first the Kingdom of God, and His righteousness; and all these things shall be added unto you.

Seek does not mean just think about it. What is the kingdom of God? "Heaven," most people would answer. Not so, says the Bible! Romans 14:17–18 reveals the actual meaning:

> For the kingdom of God is not meat and drink; but righteousness, and peace, and joy in the Holy Ghost. For he that in these things serveth Christ is acceptable to God, and approved of men.

Where do we begin to make changes so that we will not be among those who have left their first love? James 4:10 says, "Humble yourselves in the sight of the Lord, and He shall lift you up." The Greek word for *humble* is *tapeinou*, which means "to make low, debase, or lower oneself." It describes a person who is devoid of all arrogance and self-exultation—a saint who is willingly submitted to Christ and His will. This is a saint who says, "He must increase, but I must decrease" (John 3:30).

John the Baptist spoke the truth to the Jews, and this is the truth that present believers need to turn into a prayer. In prayer, tell Jesus that you are thirsty and you want Him to fill you up. Tell yourself that earthly things leave you dry and that only He can truly satisfy. Pray from your heart that all you want will be more of Him and that what you desire is to be less of yourself. You will hear Him respond in a kingdom way, which you will call foolish if you are carnal in nature instead of spiritual in nature. He will say what He has always said: you must die like a grain of wheat that falls to the earth but dies to live anew. When the grain of wheat lives anew, it grows to produce new fruit. The fruit belongs to God, not to the parent grain. The Holy Spirit will reveal to you how He sees your heart. You will either harden it in backsliding and rebellion and reap what you are sowing, or you will agree with Him and pray as Solomon did in Proverbs 21:1.

> The king's heart is in the hand of the Lord,
> as the rivers of water: He turneth it withersoever
> He will.

Ask God to turn your heart like channels of water with His own hands. Ask Him to continue and not stop until your whole life flows in the channel of His Spirit. Don't be like others who are content with a little change, like using a less vulgar vocabulary. Ask for *complete* change until your name, your life, your gifts, and your ministry all bring honor to the Lamb of God who reigns!

He will then put you to a test to see if you are sincere. He will ask you to voluntarily surrender to His work in you. Allow it or you'll be grieving the Holy Spirit of God. Then He will instruct you to rest your life within His loving hands. If you don't allow the Holy Spirit to finish this kingdom work, you'll end up as Ephraim according the prophet Hosea: "E'phraim, he hath mixed himself among the people; E'phraim is a cake not turned" (Hosea 7:8). You too will be only half useful to God. What is needed is for the other side to be turned—the whole heart changed and not just one side exposed to the Spirit. You'll need to ask the Holy Spirit to lead you to the next phase.

When He sees by your actions and reactions that you still wish to be more like Jesus, He will ask if you want to be an emptied vessel He can work through. He will ask if you desire the Refiner's fire. The evidence of being a half-baked cake like Ephraim will come when you (and others) do not love God with your "all" and do not go the distance. This means a baptism of love is needed. Don't get haughty. We all need Holy Spirit baptism again and again.

Baptized means "immersed" into something. It is not just referring to water, which is an expected step of growth following conversion. My wife and I were water baptized ten months after our conversion. So ask Jesus to immerse you in His style of loving. This is done via the Refiner's fire for the purification of the heart, not just the turning of the heart toward Him. James 4:8 says, "Draw nigh to God and he will draw nigh to you. Cleanse your hands, ye sinners; and purify your hearts, ye double-minded." The double-minded are those who sometimes love God with their "all." Doesn't God deserve more than sometimes? Yes! So pray for strength and commitment to stand when He comes. Malachi 3:2–3 says,

> But who may abide the day of His coming? And who shall stand when He appeareth? For He is like a refiner's fire, and like fuller's soap: and He shall sit as a refiner and purifier of silver: and He shall purify the sons of Levi, and purge them as gold and silver, that they may offer unto the Lord an offering in righteousness.

Do you want to be pure gold? If no is your thought and answer, then why not? Ask the Holy Spirit to convict you if it is not your heart's one desire to be set apart, sanctified—to be holy. Choose to be holy. Let Jesus be your only Master. Be ready to do His will. The cleansing will be within and not a temporary outside change. Start by not calling your negative response to God a mistake or error. Call it a sin! We must quit saying our sin is just a mistake or an unintentional oversight. No, it is not; it is a *sin*.

Many believers today (from 1995 to the present) attend churches that used to play and sing only hymns, and they looked down on the Pentecostals or charismatic churches that introduced choruses along with their hymns. However, as these "new" style churches began to outnumber the old mainline evangelical churches (not because there were more people being born again, but because the sheep were being stolen by programs, creating larger congregations that gave more money and encouraged the building of new facilities), more church boards decided to change to the "new" style of songs, which became known as "contemporary worship." Unfortunately, what started out as a biblically sound change became contaminated with New Age, non-biblical ideas coached by false teachers who said we must be blessed of God. Just look at our growth.

They began to measure growth by the number of new physical structures and the number of polled adherents instead of by the number of actual new converts. This merely represents the flow of "adherents" moving from church to church and plain old "sheep stealing" by means of promoting inter- or nondenominationalism, even at the expense of their fundamental doctrines. The instruments became electric, and the choirs evolved into worship teams. Choir robes decayed into casual attire, and hymnbooks morphed into overhead projectors and on into the computer age of PowerPoint.

This was the Ephesus church age. They loved worship and praise and what they called non-legalism more than they loved Jesus. They left their first love. They would sing about Him being worthy to receive honor and glory without studying in His Word how to worship. They didn't know what He meant when He referred to His glory or to the fact that He was and is worthy. They spoke of His great name without surrendering to Him or dying to self. Soon people were talking about how great their worship leader sang or played, and in time, the congregations worshipped the worship and not the Savior.

I challenged many pastors to change back to simpler instruments and see if the congregation still came. Were they coming to worship our Lord or just coming to a concert because they were carnal and needed to be entertained? I found no pastor willing to accept this challenge. Soon we saw coffee counters in the lobby, and then came the addition of food. It felt and looked and smelled just like going into a movie theater. Paul warned us along with the Corinthian church, "What? Have you not houses to eat and to drink in?" (1 Cor. 11:22). They had already left their first love, Jesus, for their real first love—pleasing the flesh.

In a short time, they began to ignore 1 Timothy 3:5–6, which says, "For if a man know not how to rule his own house, how shall he take care of the church of God?" The context, of course, pertains to the qualifications of a pastor. But it still applies to worship leaders, worship team members, and anyone else who dares to minister from the altar before God. In fact, many worship leaders are licensed and ordained in the music ministry. They make no secret of the fact (and some are actually proud of the fact) that they play at bars on Saturday night or at school dances on Friday nights, and then they dare to stand before the Lord of glory playing the same style with the same body language.

Their actions show that this is just another gig or venue to them, but God says this is called an offering of unholy fire. How dare they play their worldly style on an elevated platform in the house of God (which used to be called the altar, where God was met) with a pack of cigarettes in their shirt pocket. When you have left your first love, you soon forget that you were to be a priest according to biblical standards.

> "But ye are a chosen generation, a royal
> priesthood, an holy nation, a peculiar people;
> that ye should shew forth the praises of Him who

hath called you out of darkness into His marvelous light." (1 Pet. 2:9)

Find out what a priest does and does not do. Show forth the
praises of your first love instead of showing off your God-given tal-
ents. He called us out of darkness, so quit dragging darkness back
into His marvelous light. If you don't have a mature born-again guitar player (or other instrumentalist), then just wait until the King of
glory brings you one. Otherwise, beware of the consequences.

"For the time is come that judgment must
begin at the house of God: and if it first begin at
us, what shall the end be of them that obey not
the gospel of God?" (1 Pet. 4:17)

That is not an Old Testament prophet speaking but an apostle
of Jesus in the New Covenant. We have already stated that God does
not change.

"Be not deceived; God is not mocked: for
whatsoever a man soweth, that shall he also reap."
(Gal. 6:7)

The next verse tells us not to sow to the flesh. Priests are supposed to offer holy offerings to God, not unholy offerings. When
your so-called first love is replaced by questionable "worship," you
will become a priest like Nadab and Abihu, the sons of Aaron (read
Leviticus 10:1–2). As priests, they offered "strange fire." In Hebrew,
strange is *esh zuwr*, literally "of foreign." Some translate it as "profane
fire." This is a sin referred to as idolatrous worship. We've already
cited scripture (1 Samuel 15) that says stubbornness is seen by God
as idol worship. In a similar manner, today's novice or even unsaved
"worship" leaders are offering praise (fire for their censers) which
they have taken from a place other than the altar fire. The altar fire
was the only legitimate fire that could be offered to a holy God.

God loves to hear stringed instruments and drums and cymbals, but not when they sound like they came from some worldly house of worship—that is, Baal worship. Our worship cannot be stained by worldly ways. These two priests learned the hard way that God is not mocked. You don't offer God fire or offerings of praise other than that commanded by God. Why? Well... "and there went out fire from the Lord, and devoured them, and they died before the Lord" (Lev. 10:2).

Some may think that this premise is false because obviously if these offerings just mentioned had this result, then why is the fire not falling now to devour worldly priests? The answer is found in Paul's writings, where he says that the Old Testament teachings and writings are given to us for examples so that we will learn. Others would quickly say that this is just the Old Testament, and they soon forget that the same is stated in the New Testament. It's called quenching the Holy Spirit or grieving the Holy Spirit, which can lead to blaspheming the Holy Spirit—the unforgiveable sin. Therefore, the fire falls but to our thinking it is delayed. The delayed fire is eternal judgment since that sin cannot be forgiven.

Just look around the USA, and see how our unchangeable God is trying to get His church and His people to repent before further judgment falls. The only solution for this shameful sin of leaving your first love is for the church and individuals to admit that it is a sin against God's holiness and integrity. We will be forgiven: "if we confess our sins, He is faithful and just to forgive us our sins, and to cleanse us from all unrighteousness" (1 John 1:9). Next, we must do as Jesus told the woman taken in adultery. The scribes and Pharisees wanted to stone her, but Jesus said "Neither do I condemn thee: go, and sin no more" (John 8:11).

Now pray for the turning of heart that calls out for an experience that only the hand of a majestic, authoritative, yet tenderhearted and assisting Savior is able to give. Pray to Jesus that He will give you a longing that only He can fill. You need a stronger longing than you have ever experienced even in your dreams—not like the striking of a single match but like the blazing of a forest fire out of control. That can only be calmed by Christ alone.

Now you know that it's possible for even the elect to leave their first love and how unprofitable it would be for you and those in your small sphere of influence to do so, you must call out to the King of glory to take you deeper in love with Him and out of love with yourself and anything that is not Him. Long for it as David wrote in Psalm 42:1.

As the hart panteth after the water brooks,
so panteth my soul after thee, O God.

In the next chapter, we will discuss what is needed to make room in your heart for more of Him and the obstacles that prohibit a deeper love of Him. It won't be easy, and it is always painful; but as the hymn writer says, "It will be worth it all when we see Jesus."

5
This Laodicean-Age Church
Is a Real Problem

Jesus, in His messages to the seven churches in the Book of Revelation, has not one good thing to say about this church age. Yes, it was a real church in Asia Minor with great commercial prosperity, much like the USA. It also had a rich banking center, much like that in America.

> Because thou sayest, I am rich, and increased with goods, and have need of nothing; and knowest not that thou art wretched, and miserable, and poor, and blind, and naked. (Rev. 3:17)

These seven messages are thought to represent seven church eras, especially by those who study the branch of theology called eschatology. This study concerns itself with end times subjects taught in the Bible, usually by trying to examine prophetic scriptures to see how they are being, or have been, fulfilled by current events. Many believe, as I do, that the church is living in this last era now. Nobody knows when it will end, but we are told to be watching and to be ready. The climax will be the return of Jesus, our King, to the planet earth. The last seven years of the Laodicean church age is called the Great Tribulation as mentioned in the Book of Revelation.

Jesus has no commendations for our church age. This age does not reject evil, has no patience, doesn't gracefully bear sufferings, keeps faith in faith rather than in Christ, and doesn't persevere in the faith as the previous church age did. This church age is indifferent and refuses to receive Christ's instruction to repent and to be zealous. Although some individuals attempt to be faithful, many churches participate in Halloween, celebrate the Easter bunny, and refer to Santa Claus as if he is equal with Jesus.

When I was a pastor in Idaho, I was connected with the local pregnancy center. Many of the pastors gave counsel and prayer, but three-fourths of the teenage girls came from the largest church youth group in this town of 30,000 people. While attending a yearly district convention, I was told by the motel manager that he was happy to host housing for the district conventions because during those events, he rented out more R- and X-rated movies than during any other big meetings. And most of those conventions were attended by husbands and wives together!

Our two sons attended a Christian high school, and I would sometimes attend basketball games. In the stands, one could not tell that there were any Christians involved with this school. The comments sounded as negative as any heard at a public-school game, especially those directed at the referees. Before I was called into the ministry, I had worked with a couple of the referees, and they had told me at work how difficult it was. "I thought Christians would be different," they said as they smirked at the phony Christian parents while I could only weep, as I still do.

The danger of being lukewarm, for which Jesus rebuked the Laodiceans, is that you are in a rocking-chair state—you are going to sleep, back and forth, back and forth, and not doing anything really evil but not doing anything that mirrors Christ. You are just going along with the crowd, saying there's nothing wrong with cancelling Sunday evening service on Super Bowl Sunday so you can invite your un-churched friends over for chili and the game. Pastors see this phenomenon at other times of the year as well. It was always a weeping moment for me when deer hunting season opened and a large percentage of believers were not in attendance at church.

Some pastors give up and say, "That's okay. We'll just be a 'hunter's church,' a 'golf church,' a 'cowboy church,' or a 'fishing church.'" None of this thinking would have been tolerated during the Philadelphia church age. The church persevered in the faith during the American Civil War and through any other calamity that came up. Christ had no criticism of them. He instructed them to keep the faith, and they obeyed. He promised them a place in God's presence, a new name, and the gift of the New Jerusalem. That is why I have decided to be a Philadelphia-type church member, living in the Laodicean age.

How do you do that, you may ask? You must want truth rather than tickled ears from loving those false teachers and hirelings.

> Jesus sayeth unto him, I am the way, the truth, and the life: no man cometh unto the Father, but by me. (John 14:6)

He did not say *a* truth, but *the* truth—not one of many truths but the *only* truth! Why is that so uniquely important? The truth gives freedom from non-truth traps, snares, lies, and glittering temptations that hold us in bondage. The truth of One who cannot lie allows a born-again Christian of the Laodicean age to see these rocking chair enticements as they really are: tools of Satan. The antichrist system will lead you to the lake of fire. We must seek after the totality of the truth: Jesus himself as a person, not just an idea. But we cannot overlook additional kingdom truths.

> And it is the Spirit that beareth witness, because the Spirit is truth. (1 John 5:6)

This is the Holy Spirit. He, not *it*, is the third part of the Trinity. God, the Father, gives revelation truth to those who humbly serve Him. Jacob realized that God was ordering his life:

> I am not worthy of the least of all the mercies, and of all the truth, which Thou hast shewed

unto Thy servant; for with my staff I passed over this Jordan; and now I am become two bands. (Gen. 32:10)

And Moses sings the truth of God:

He is the Rock, His work is perfect: for all His ways are judgment: a God of truth and without iniquity, just and right is He. (Deut. 32:4)

God's words, His commandments, are truth. Don't ever neglect the reading or hearing of God's holy Word.

Thou art near, O Lord; and all Thy commandments are truth. (Ps. 119:151)

It is extremely important that we recognize one of the problems of the Laodicean age is that the so-called believers agree with the Scriptures when they are confronted or involved in discussions about verses, but they do not fully believe and have faith that the Scriptures say exactly what God means and that it has not changed. This was seen in the recent pandemic, when the hirelings who "careth not for the sheep," saw a wolf disguised as a virus, and closed and locked the doors of their churches. They were walking by sight and not by faith. Their sight told them the virus had more power than their God. Their reasoning might be Romans 13, forgetting or perhaps never having been acquainted with Acts 5:29.

Then Peter and the other apostles answered and said, "We ought to obey God rather than men."

We do obey the civil authorities until their decisions run contrary to the Word of God. This is typical of a lukewarm Laodicean-age church. They seem to have forgotten how popular the book (by Corrie ten Boom) and movie *The Hiding Place* were and have also forgotten how many agreed with the ten Boom's actions in defending themselves against anti-Christian/anti-Jewish civil authorities.

The Philadelphia saint is given experiences allowed and engineered by God to show us His mercy, love, and ability to care for His children. We never rely on self, for we have learned we are not dependable and we will reap woes if we rely on ourselves. We ask for the Holy Spirit to draw us and give us the ability to obey and follow where He leads us.

> Thy word is a lamp unto my feet, and a
> light unto my path. (Ps. 119:105)

He is not referring to commentary notes or other so-called biblical helps printed in our Bibles. Recently we experienced this when a Sunday school teacher spent the whole class hour using his personal journal notations, but there was not one single Bible verse. The oil of God's lamp is Holy Spirit truth, which inspired the writing of the Bible.

How do we mature to this level of pleasing God? After falling deeper in love with Him, we learn that God inhabits the praises of His people. (Ps. 22:3). Out of love for Him, we would praise Him even if He didn't promise to inhabit, but we knew that verse and believed it: "But Thou art holy, O Thou that inhabitest the praises of Israel." With God, the great, powerful, and mighty Creator walking next to us as our shield and fortress, we fear not what man can do to us. Paul warned us about this when he wrote his second letter to Timothy (2 Timothy 3:12): "Yea, and all that will live godly in Christ Jesus, shall suffer persecution." If you are not suffering persecution, either you are not a Christian, or you are not walking or living godly in Christ Jesus. But for those who are, the truth of Psalm 22:3 becomes a reality. Why? Because nobody messes with the Rock of my Salvation, my Shelter in a time of storm.

Yes, God is omnipresent. But what you need is God's manifested omnipresence. Start praising Him without trying to treat Him as your personal butler or some carnival show dog. Always keep these in mind:

> For with God nothing shall be impossible."
> (Luke 1:37)

> Now unto Him that is able to do exceed-
> ing abundantly above all that we ask or think,
> according to the power that worketh in us, unto
> Him be glory in the church by Christ Jesus
> throughout all ages, world without end. Amen."
> (Eph. 3:20–21)

The walk of faith, not by sight or self-guidance, brought us to falling deeper in love with Jesus and out of love with everything else. The result was dying to selfish ambitions and growing new ambitions to please God as the Holy Spirit drew us to this truth: "But without faith it is impossible to please Him: for he that cometh to God must believe that He is, and that He is a rewarder of them that diligently seek Him" (Heb. 11:6). Diligently seeking is not just going to church, praying, and reading the Bible. We are talking about a steadfastness of believing in all that He is and promises to do. The Greek word *ekzeteo*, used for *diligently*, means "to seriously investi-gate and crave satisfaction in the searching out of an issue." We don't do anything halfway or sloppy as His priests. God in turn tells us how to increase our faith.

> So then faith cometh by hearing, and hear-
> ing by the word of God. (Rom. 10:17)

This does not say *reading*. It says *hearing*. It is not hearing some-one "read" the Bible to you. We already have said that the sheep know His voice. You need to put yourself in the position to hear God's voice, His Word. He will either speak directly to you, indirectly through a pastor who has received a teaching ministry, through an angel, through the gift of tongues with interpretations, through the gift of prophecy, or through (this is the one we don't like) teaching and testing as in Job-like experiences. Many times, God will allow a testing experience to show us whether we have learned what He wants us to know. He already knows whether we have learned it or not, but we don't.

> Many are the afflictions of the righteous,
> but the Lord delivereth him out of them all. (Ps. 34:19)

The adherents at Ephesus and Laodicea made the mistake of substituting words. This is one of the ongoing problems in the church today. God said in Psalm 34:19, "the Lord delivers." When we use the word *Lord*, it means we have made Him our lord, so He has lordship over us. A heart change is only the first step for us. Next, after we have our love in the right order, we must go to Hebrews 12 and look at verse 1:

> Let us lay aside every weight, and the sin
> which doth so easily beset us, and let us run with
> patience the race that is set before us.

Ask the Holy Spirit what besetting sin you have. Don't ask yourself. We usually lie to ourselves. Once He tells you what it is (or what they are), ask for Holy Spirit help and strength. Soon He will tell you, "Be still, and know that I am God: I will be exalted among the heathen, I will be exalted in the earth" (Ps. 46:10). You will receive revealed truth to help you understand—know. It will involve experiencing regular times of silent waiting and expectant tranquility. Look at the many examples God has provided for His people:

> And Moses said unto the people, 'Fear
> ye not, stand still and see the salvation of the
> Lord, which he will show to you today: for the
> Egyptians whom ye have seen today, ye shall see
> them again no more forever. (Exod. 14:13)

Egypt represents slavery and bondage for the Christian. *Salvation* is the word here for deliverance. The problem then and now is that people murmur; and instead of remembering that God has already said, "*Be still,*" they try to be wise in their own eyes, thinking that they can solve their problems without God's help.

Psalm 46:10 says to do two things: (1) quit making noise over what you think is right or about "your plans," and just listen; (2) know that "I am God." To know is not to read about, pretend to know about, or even to know *about* God. It is to know God—to personally know Him, who holds your next breath. God will do things His way, as always, which most of us are uncomfortable with or even unable to tolerate. Acts 14:22 confirms "that we must through much tribulation enter into the kingdom of God." I bet you didn't get up early or wait in line to hear or read that truth!

So the question must be: after salvation, where do we start to be still? James 3 tells us about the problem with our tongue, even calling it an unruly evil. The tongue problem is solved by: (1) changing our environment, friends, and contact with family members who are not saved; (2) having our heart turned to Him to flow in His river of grace; and (3) allowing God to renew our minds. First Corinthians 15:33 says, "Do not be deceived: evil communications corrupt good manners." The Holy Spirit inspired Paul to show that our lives are influenced by what we believe *and* with whom we associate.

God has inspired Paul to write, "I beseech you, therefore, brethren…" Stop right there! *Brethren* refers to the saints—then, today, and tomorrow. He continues, "By the mercies of God, that ye…" Stop again, and pay attention. He continues, "present your bodies…" And who should do that? All who call themselves believers, even the Laodiceans. He continues, "A living sacrifice, holy, acceptable unto God." Stop! He means we are to be a living sacrifice to God, measuring up to the standard that God says is acceptable as an offering. How do we know what is acceptable?

> Study to show thyself approved unto God, a
> workman that needeth not to be ashamed, rightly
> dividing the word of truth." (2 Tim. 2:15)

Get away from these hirelings who give you a thirty-minute sermonette filled with ten minutes of commercials and introduction, a few humorous stories, ten to fifteen minutes of baby food, and follow with the conclusion review. Think back to Romans 12:1, which says, "Which is your reasonable service." Pay close attention to verse 2: "And be not conformed to this world: but be ye transformed…" Now stop again! How do we do that? "By the renewing of your mind…" Why? "That ye may prove what is that good and acceptable, and perfect will of God." Laodicean saints don't do this because they want their desire, not God's. They love the world and try hard to conform to it. They have lost their fear—respect and standing in awe—of God, so they make excuses for not obeying.

> Love not the world, neither the things that are in the world. If any man love the world the love of the Father is not in him. For all that is in the world, the lust of the flesh, and the lust of the eyes, and the pride of life, is not of the Father but is of the world. (1 John 2:15–16)

Repentance is the only way to solve this problem. Then we begin to renew the mind.

> Finally, brethren, whatsoever things are true, whatsoever things are honest, whatsoever things are just, whatsoever things are pure, whatsoever things are lovely, whatsoever things are of good report; if there be any virtue, and if there be any praise, <u>think</u> on these things. (Phil. 4:8)

Did you notice that all of these subjects that we are to think on are truths of Jesus? One could substitute the name of Christ for each word. But if you don't have a change of heart, all you'll do is use the old earthly, unspiritual way of thinking about the words *pure* or *of good report* or any of the other words in this text. Always ask for Holy

Spirit revelation and illumination regarding concepts that come from the kingdom of God.

The first thing you'll realize is that the new you is not the same person as the old you.

> Therefore if any man be in Christ, he is a
> new creature: old things are passed away; behold,
> all things are become new. (2 Cor. 5:17)

The English word *new* is *kainos* in Greek. It means "fresh, nothing ever before like it." It is not like painting your wall to make it look different. Paint has been on it before. But it's more like putting on wallpaper where wallpaper has never been heard of before. It isn't just changing the color of something, but it's actually a different substance. The new creature in Christ—you—now has a desire and ability to see things in a more God-like way. You'll want to gaze at or set your spiritual eyes on Jesus, the Lord of your life. You'll desire like never before to see His face. Then because you've had purification of heart and a turning of your heart toward Him, you'll want to be as close to the Bridegroom as the bride is, in order to hear His heartbeat. Then you'll realize that your heart is beating with His, the two hearts beating as one heart. He will say to you, "Follow Me," and you won't hesitate. You will respond out of a new love for Him, saying, "I'll follow faithfully." Then you'll see a small tear come down His lovely face, much like when He wept over Jerusalem. You'll ask respectfully, "Why are you crying?"

And He will respond this way: "Can two walk together except they be agreed?" (Amos 3:3).

You'll ask, "How are we not agreed, Lord?"

He'll say tenderly, "You still haven't laid aside each weight of bondage. You're not allowing Me as your Shepherd, to use My rod and staff to comfort you. These were meant for you so that you may see My holiness and My righteousness. You thank Me for inviting you into My family. You give Me conditional praise, but there's so much more."

You can test yourself to see if your heart has been changed, to see if you are a new creature in Christ. Do you still long to make contact with, talk with, go with, be entertained with or by, "have fun" with, and participate in the same things that your old friends and contacts participated in? If you do, you are not a new creature in Christ. You are an old creature in self instead of new in Christ. If you call yourself a Christian and still do and think the old, carnal way (the way of your old life and friends), you are in danger of being vomited out of Jesus's mouth. This is not a good state to be in when Jesus returns—you will be left behind like the unwise virgins. The only solution is to repent and be converted.

The Ephesian- and Laodicean-type church folks never grow to these levels. Look at the Laodiceans in Revelation 3. Because of their self-interest, they didn't know that they were wretched and blind. Jesus wishes to have them (us) ask to have an anointing of eye salve so that they (we) may see. That area of Asia Minor was noted for being a banking center and for the production of a glossy black wool used in clothing and carpets. All of these are examples of the pride of life; and all of them are saying, "Look at me and what I have done!" These are not sinful things unless they cause you to make them your gods. Jesus says, "Toss them aside." The Laodiceans were also known for producing a salve for the curing of eye disorders. Anyone who has adopted the philosophy of the original Laodicean church, regardless of the geographical area in which they live and regardless of what year it is on the calendar, will desperately need a revival of grace in which the eyes of their hearts are Holy Spirit illuminated. Then they will be able to say without shame, "No matter what God is doing in me, even if I can't see it or realize it, I'll still say, 'So be it!'"

Idol worship is a huge problem in American churches today (1945–present). We don't call our idols Baal, but they are just the same and do as much damage. We worship our work, education, sports, achievements, and even churches. In years past, when I went reluctantly to sectional or district conventions, I would sooner or later hear someone saying, "Oh, you only have 100 members in your church? We've been so blessed. We're running 650–700 with multiple services" blah, blah, blah… They forget that some of the deeper teachings of Jesus were only shared with Peter, James, and John. Nine hundred people didn't see the transfiguration!

Church and youth groups can also be idols. So what needs to be done about this? We need Holy Spirit conviction and repentance. What we need is not manmade holy laughter but real holy weeping. God said, "If My people, which are called by My name, shall humble themselves, and pray, and seek My face, and *turn from their wicked ways; then* will I hear from heaven, and will forgive their sin, and will heal their land" (2 Chron. 7:14). We have to do our part first. God is not obligated to respond in a favorable way if we refuse to obey Him. Spiritual pride is an idol. Remember how God deals with pride:

> Pride goeth before destruction, and an haughty spirit before a fall. (Prov. 16:18)

> But the proud He knoweth afar off. (Ps. 138:6)

You cannot hear His heartbeat unless you are close to Him.

> For God resisteth the proud, and giveth grace to the humble. (1 Pet. 5:5)

Tell me, fellow believers, do you really want the great Almighty God to be against you, resisting you? What can we do? First, realize this truth: "My times are in Thy hand..." (Ps. 31:15). Ask God to teach you how to see that each man has only so many minutes, days, and years. We must use them wisely, honoring Him, "redeeming the time, because the days are evil" (Eph. 5:16). Simply put, this means buying up every opportunity for service to the King.

As you grow deeper in love with God and His ways and teachings, and out of love with yourself and the world, you will have an intense interest and attraction for God as David wrote in Psalm 27:4,

> One thing have I desired of the Lord, that will I seek after; that I may dwell in the house

of the Lord all the days of my life, to behold the
beauty of the Lord, and to inquire in His temple.

The *beauty* in Hebrew is *no am*, meaning "splendor" or "pleas-
antness." This surpasses anything man can accomplish or make or do.
Keep growing and you'll not be like the Christians mentioned earlier,
but you'll soon be enraptured by His unequalled love for you as if you
were the only human being He died for. After a while, you'll enter
into the realm of spiritual activity stimulated by His glory, which will
one day cover the earth: "but as truly as I live, all the earth shall be
filled with the glory of the Lord" (Num. 14:21). The Hebrew word
for *glory* is *kabod*, meaning "splendor." Those who have experienced
this liberation declare unashamedly that our God is worthy of praise
and honor and love and obedience! Or, as the hymn writer has said,
"Oh, for a thousand tongues to sing my great Redeemer's praise!"

If you always just sing that great Charles Wesley hymn from the
book, note by note, and not from your heart—you're just another
Laodicean, and Jesus is knocking on the door of your heart trying
to get in. America is home to a complacent, self-satisfied church
because of compromise from the pulpit. Your self-satisfaction is what
keeps Jesus knocking, but with lawlessness running rampant, very
few believers realize that the Lord of glory needs to rule from inside
the heart.

> Lift up your heads, O ye gates; and be ye
> lift up ye everlasting doors; and the King of glory
> shall come in. (Ps. 24:7)

The result will be that you will see what David proclaimed in
Psalm 63:3–4: "Because Thy loving kindness is better than life, my
lips shall praise Thee." Look at the next verse for a demonstrative
love: "Thus will I bless Thee while I live: I will lift up my hands in
Thy name." The Laodiceans claim they don't add or subtract from
the Bible, and they freely quote Revelation 22:18–19.

> If any man shall add unto these things, God shall add unto him the plagues that are written in this book: And if any man shall take away from the words of the book of this prophecy, God shall take away his part out of the book of life, and out of the holy city, and from the things which are written in this book.

But they claim it only refers to the Book of Revelation. Oh, really? How about Deuteronomy 4:2?

> Ye shall not add unto the word which I command you, neither shall ye diminish ought from it, that ye may keep the commandments of the Lord your God which I command you.

And there is Proverbs 30:6, written long after Moses wrote the first five books:

> Add thou not unto His words lest He reprove thee, and thou be found a liar.

In which ways then are the hirelings and Laodiceans adding (or more often, subtracting) from God's Word? We just read how David lifted up his hands, but we don't see this act of worship in very many non-Pentecostal or non-charismatic churches today as they ignore 1 Timothy 2:8, which says, "I will therefore that men pray everywhere, lifting up holy hands, without wrath and doubting." This was customary among the Jews and even the heathens. The hands were lifted and spread out toward heaven as a posture of surrender.

Similarly, the Laodiceans have added to Psalm 47:1, which Timothy knew from a young age, "O clap your hands, all ye people; shout unto God with the voice of triumph." They have basically changed that to, "We are Baptist, Church of Christ, or Lutheran, and we don't do this Pentecostal kind of worship. We only shout at basketball games and football games." Psalm 47:1 said *all*, not only the youth or the Pentecostals. This is an example of "church" becoming an idol as we practice denominationalism instead of obeying God. An example of judgment for "taking away" from God's Word is seen in Jeremiah 36:20–32. Read it and weep.

This verse will bring us to what we must do without delay. Satan, the flesh, the world, and even the lukewarm will mock you and say you are being legalistic. No! You must be Bible-istic! Say and do this out of love for your Redeemer, your Savior, your Friend, your only God, and your constant Companion: "Lord Jesus, I will bow to You, the Lover of my soul, because You are so good even when I'm not. I will worship by choice and no longer be a spectator on the sidelines. I will lay down my idols, my ambitions and desires, my plans, all things made by my hands, and my mind. I will tear down thrones I have made and phony, lying kings I have enthroned. I will remove them and put You on the throne of my heart. I will freely admit that these things have taken my heart, which belongs to You and You alone. I want to be in the grip of Your compassion." Ask the Holy Spirit to burn in your heart the new desire to say, "All I desire is You," and to make Jesus more precious to you than silver and gold.

From this point on, I want you to compare some scriptures. First, let's look at the very positive verse 1 Corinthians 2:9.

> But as it is written, Eye hath not seen, nor ear heard, neither have entered into the heart of man, the things which God hath prepared for them that love him.

I don't know about you, but I've seen some impressive sights. And heaven is better. I've heard about some adventures that make me dream. But heaven is better. And how about this one in Colossians 3:1–2?

> If ye then be risen with Christ, seek those things which are above, where Christ sitteth on the right hand of God. Set your affection on things above, not on things on the earth.

And apply those two truths with this additional verse:

> The Spirit itself beareth witness with our
> spirit, that we are the children of God: and if
> children, then heirs; heirs of God, and joint-heirs
> with Christ; if so be that we suffer with Him,
> that we may be also glorified together; For I
> reckon that the sufferings of this present time are
> not worthy to be compared with the glory which
> shall be revealed in us. (Rom. 8:16–18)

Now go back, and read those verses again; but this time do it
not as though you are reading a newspaper or magazine or bulletin.
This time, ask for Holy Spirit illumination and revelation. Then consider these negative comparisons.

> But the fearful, and unbelieving, and the
> abominable, and murderers, and whoremongers,
> and sorcerers, and idolaters, and all liars, shall
> have their part in the lake which burneth with
> fire and brimstone: which is the second death.
> (Rev. 21:8)

> But the heavens and the earth, which are
> now, by the same word are kept in store, reserved
> unto fire against the day of judgment and perdi-
> tion of ungodly men. (2 Pet. 3:7)

These comparisons must be meditated upon and not just read
in passing.

The decision is clear for all but the "Ephesus" Christian and
the "Laodicean" Christian. The "Philadelphia-type" believer cries out
unashamedly, "All I desire is You." He knows that there are no riches
on the earth that compare to the glorious King of kings, Jesus! Now
tell me, Friend, what can this world and its systems offer? You read
the outcome. Are you doubtful? No one can cheer your heart like

Jesus. Is the Almighty God your Redeemer, your only hiding place, and your safe refuge? He can be—if you ask Him to be all this for you. Start delighting yourself in Him. We all become weak at times, but He makes us strong.

> And He said unto me, "My grace is suffi-
> cient for thee: for My strength is made perfect
> in weakness. Most gladly therefore will I rather
> glory in my infirmities, that the power of Christ
> may rest upon me." (2 Cor. 12:9)

Don't listen to your flesh or to the father of lies. Our God is Almighty and most holy. He is faithful through the ages. Stake a claim on the promises of God, and seal them in faith. Who shall be exalted? Whose kingdom shall not pass away? The Ancient of days! Look at Psalm 139:14. Does your soul know that very well? If not, get out of that lukewarm church before Christ vomits you out of His mouth. When you begin to see the very things you thought were stable falling away, then the remnant church will still stand. How? Only by the power of His hand. Ask God to have mercy on your situation, and plead for revival in your own heart and in your city and country. Ask God to break the spiritual chains by releasing His power.

What the church needs is true teaching on adoration and standing in reverent awe. Do you consider yourself to be one of the sons of the Almighty? Then give back to the Lord glory and strength that's due only to Him. Our God said, "For thou shalt worship no other god: for the Lord whose name is Jealous, is a jealous God" (Exod. 34:14). This covenant name is *qana* from the root *qanna*, which means "to make jealous or envious" or "to provoke to jealousy." We, His children, therefore need to follow David's request: "O magnify the Lord with me, and let us exalt His name together" (Ps. 34:3). Every thought you have about God, every truth revealed to you, needs to be made *larger*, magnified!

God is not a capricious plaything. He doesn't have erratic behavior, nor does He have a whimsical personality. Does the omnipotent Father of power and strength control your personal universe? Why?

Or why not? Do you proclaim Him as the only God of the earth? Start allowing our awesome God to reign with His wisdom, power, and love in your life. Don't be a Laodicean church member! They made God too small in their eyes, and that is why He tells them to use a different anointing eye salve. Failing to respond to this God is a sin.

Ask Jesus to forgive you for this sin. Quit believing the lies that you think and hear—that He is not able to help you. Admit that this attitude has wounded your heart, and ask Him to heal it. Quit leaning on the wisdom of men, including yourself; and quit responding to them. Too many people treat other people as gods. Stop it! Call it a sin and repent. The result will be refreshing springs of peace that will be comforting to your troubled soul. This doesn't mean you won't be in yet another spiritual battle, but God wishes us to be still and realize there is just one thing we need right now: we need to hear the soft voice of our Lord. His guidance is still available if we will repent.

There is still a river of grace for us to plunge into, so do it! His strong arms are still longing to embrace you. He can do this because He is eternal, and we are but a moment. Learn this when you are broken: "For he knoweth our frame; he remembereth that we are dust" (Ps. 103:14). Read the entire chapter, and bring a box of tissues with you. Continue to bow your heart before Him. Continue to worship and adore Him and not only during Christmas and Easter. Our God is perfect in every way. Ask yourself if you are a willing servant or if you are putting up conditional parameters to keep Him at a distance.

Of course, the thing we all need to do as Christians is ask for the Holy Spirit to burn out the dross in our lives until we have become the sacrifice we are called to be, consumed by the Lord. Always remember this fire is an act of love; it is the fire of the Holy One. We have a part in becoming a holy priesthood. We have to allow the Holy Spirit to cast down our vain imaginations. Otherwise, we will build a "calf" like Aaron did, excusing himself as a "weak" man. What a poor excuse for giving in to the vain imaginations of the crowd! These vain imaginations usually exalt themselves. Please, O God, cause a holy hunger in us. Jesus said, "Blessed (to be envied) are they which do hunger and thirst after righteousness; for they shall be filled." Simply put, where there is no hunger and no thirst, there is no filling.

The Laodiceans today do hunger, but they forget to wait on the Lord. This lost generation wants instant gratification and praise for themselves whether they have earned it or not. After all, since they were two or three years old, they've heard "Good job!" from parents, grandparents, day care workers, and teachers.

> Wait on the Lord: be of good courage and
> He shall strengthen thine heart: wait, I say, on
> the Lord! (Ps. 27:14)

When waiting, rest in faith, and listen to His voice. When we put our own effort and labor ahead of waiting for the Lord, failure will be the result.

> *Except* the Lord build the house, they labor
> in vain that build it: except the Lord keep the city,
> the watchman waketh but in vain. (Ps. 127:1)

It makes a difference when we do all things the Lord's way. It doesn't matter whether it is in a church, business, or your home and life. It makes a difference!

It makes a difference where you start. Isaiah 28:16 says, "Therefore thus saith the Lord God, Behold, I lay in Zion for a foundation a stone, a tried stone, a precious corner stone, a sure foundation; he that believeth shall not make haste." Peter verifies in 1 Peter 2:6 that Jesus is that cornerstone. If you are still struggling to receive this truth, then do as David did: "Search me, O God, and know my heart: try me, and know my thoughts: and see if there be any wicked way in me, and lead me in the way everlasting" (Ps. 139:23–24).

David wants God to show him how he has missed the mark. He is not trying to justify himself. You have no reason to regret asking God or to fear His answer if you do, so call on Him. His love for you won't change. He is our constant companion and best friend.

He never sleeps or goes on a vacation. He will whisper to your heart whether it is early in the morning or late in the evening.

How will you realize this? What action is our loving Lord allowing us to take? Admit that your days are few and pass quickly. Ask Jesus to draw you very close to Him. When this happens your heart and His will beat together and you will receive God-given revelation like a flood of water. It will be like a floodlight hitting a dark room. Then Heaven's grace and His light will change you. This is beyond your initial salvation experience and soon His purposes and plans for your life will become clear. Why? He will give spiritual eyes that allow you to see with His sight.

> For now we see through a glass, darkly; but then face to face: now I know in part; but then I shall know even as also I am known. (1 Cor. 13:12)

Pray for the loosening of the Holy Spirit's wind that brings heaven's change. When you arrive at this level of spiritual growth—or as the Bible says, "From glory to glory He changes me"—think of yourself on the Sea of Galilee. Sometimes on the shore, it is still; but other times, it is storm blown. The same thing happens when you are out on the sea, but you are in a boat with a sail. Before you go out to the sea, you need to mend the sail, patch over holes, and make the boat seaworthy. When the wind of the Holy Spirit starts to blow, don't lower the sail. It's not a storm that will blow you off course or sink you. It will be a guiding wind, a comforting wind, a wind for accomplishing some task God has allowed you to do for His service. Put up the largest sail possible to catch all of the Holy Spirit wind. That is catching the wind that brings heaven's change.

6

How to Gracefully Bear Suffering and Be Faithful until Death or the Rapture

The title of this chapter is the commendation and instruction Jesus gave to the church at Smyrna. This church and the one at Philadelphia are the only two churches Christ did not criticize.

One of the scriptures that I believe is given to pastors is found in 2 Corinthians 11:2.

> For I am jealous over you with godly jeal-
> ousy: for I have espoused you to one husband,
> that I may present you as a chaste virgin to Christ.

The genuine under-shepherds need to be jealous, like God is, because there are so many false gods and religious hirelings within the church trying to woo the sheep to their death march. Paul said that the one husband of the church is Christ, married to the one bride, the church; and it is a marriage of a holy relationship. But take warning! Matthew 25:2 tells of ten virgins: "And five of them were wise and five were foolish." However, both groups are virgins going forth to meet Jesus, the Bridegroom. The problem is that the foolish were focused on other cares, and so they did not check their oil supply and took no extra oil in their lamps. Not so for the wise. Verse 6 tells us Jesus, the Bridegroom, tarried until midnight. He was coming for those who loved Him enough to wait, watch, and be ready. The foolish went out to buy oil—a big mistake! And the result is in verses 10–12:

> And while they went to buy, the bridegroom came; and they that were ready went in with him to the marriage: and the door was shut. Afterward came also the other virgins, saying, Lord, Lord, open to us. But he answered and said, Verily I say unto you, I know you not.

Pay close attention to verse 13: "Watch therefore, for ye know neither the day nor the hour wherein the Son of man cometh." So which are you? The five wise equal 50 percent of the church, but there remains the 50 percent unwise. Which group are we truthfully in? And who are the wise? The answer has been told in the first five chapters of this book: the unwise are likened to the churches of Ephesus and Laodicea.

Jesus deserves a bride who is full of faith and not tainted by the stains of this world. That means they think like, look like, and behave like Jesus; they do not think like, look like, or behave like the foolish of this world. Now who do you think came up with the idea of tattoos? Do you think it was the world or the Christians? Who came up with the idea of piercing the body, lips, ears, nose, etc.? Do you think it was the world or the church? And who came up with the great idea of wearing flip-flops and shorts, drinking coffee and eating during/in the service? Do you think it was the world or the Christians?

I give latitude to new Christians who come to church as God's newly adopted babes. But if you've been born again for three or four years, and you still act like you did when you were first saved, then you are in danger of being in the 50 percent who are unwise. For your sake, I hope I am wrong! But that's not a gamble I'm willing to take. Nor was it the belief of those men of God mentioned earlier, whom we call our church fathers.

The church of Smyrna suffered because they would not compromise on the teachings of Christ and the apostles. They were persecuted, laughed at, and endured blasphemous remarks. Jesus told them not to fear such things: "For God hath not given us the spirit of fear; but of power, and of love, and of a sound mind" (2 Tim. 1:7). The English phrase "sound mind" in Greek is *sophranismas*. It comes from two words: *sos*, meaning "safe," and *phren*, meaning the "mind." Together, these make a word that means a safe-thinking calmness and a well-balanced, disciplined mind. It is a gift from God which comes via grace and declaration from His throne.

The church at Smyrna received this gift by positioning themselves in the proper location to receive it. They obeyed the words of John 2:15 and did not love the world or the things of the world. They learned the truth of Hebrews 11:6, which says, "But without faith it is impossible to please Him: for he that cometh to God must believe that He is, and that He is a rewarder of them that diligently seek Him." To gain faith, they got closer to His heart, and the result is revealed in Romans 10:17: "So then faith cometh by hearing, and hearing by the word of God." If you are closer to Him, you will find it much easier to hear Him.

This growth of faith allows you to take your stand like Daniel in the lion's den or Hananiah, Mishael, and Azariah when they faced the burning fiery furnace. The unwise do not receive this needed faith, but the wise do receive it and make use of it. Why is this so important? Jesus asked this question: "I tell you that He will avenge them speedily. Nevertheless when the Son of man come, shall He find faith on the earth?" This question is written in the highest Greek and with such grammar as to signify that the answer to the question is *no*. The Smyrna-type saint of God (remember, *saint* means "called-out one" and does not refer to someone who has accomplished great deeds or works for humanity) was full of faith even during persecution. Those believers reflected their Father, Yahweh.

> Know therefore that the Lord, thy God, He
> is God, the faithful God, which keepeth cove-
> nant and mercy with them that love Him and

keep His commandments to a thousand generations. (Deut. 7:9)

I hope you caught the necessary prerequisite for the great I AM
to show His faithfulness. He is faithful even if we don't do our part,
but in order to see His faithfulness demonstrated, we have to first
love Him and second, keep His commandments. The Smyrna-type
Christian does this and realizes that God is a faithful God. God
becomes the role model in his eyes. Otherwise, when persecution
comes, the believer would be in despair. But God is faithful; and He
gives you a reward for your faith in the form of His mercy and good-
ness with the knowledge that one day, you will see His glory. Our
faithful Father has said, "For I know the thoughts that I think toward
you, saith the Lord, thoughts of peace, and not of evil, to give you an
expected end" (Jer. 29:11).

And these next few verses go on to tell us that God uses strategic
timing in His plan. He uses this to fulfill His promises. He fulfills
His word and promises because God does not lie—He cannot lie,
and He is not able to lie. Whatever He chooses to do and however He
fulfills these promises in connection with His purposes is in response
to the prayers of His faithful people. They have been through the fire
and will be snatched off this planet and changed in the twinkling of
an eye.

> Behold, I shew you a mystery; We shall
> not all sleep [die], but we shall all be changed,
> in a moment, in the twinkling of an eye, at the
> last trump, for the trumpet shall sound, and the
> dead shall be raised incorruptible, and we shall be
> changed. (1 Cor. 15:51-52)

Those who are wise are as close to the Bridegroom as possible
and have learned through the water and the fire that their Deliverer
is faithful to lead them on. They know He is more than able to keep
them strong enough to be finishers. He is the leader, and He walks

before them as the Light of the World. He is guiding them home to the place He has prepared—a place like nothing seen or heard before.

This growth of faith all originates from the power of His love. His love is exactly what shed His blood. The Smyrna Christians are faithful to allow their hearts to be changed and renewed gladly, excitedly receiving His free grace that is never stagnant. Stagnation causes death as seen in the Dead Sea. It can never support life like the Sea of Galilee. Soon these faithful begin to like what they've come to know via revelation truth. They have learned and believe that all the failures and weaknesses they recognize in themselves will be stripped away by His touch of love, and they will no longer make excuses for them. They must get close to Him.

Pray this as the Smyrna saints do, that you will be held close and allow His agape love to surround you. The result is that you will learn to wait because of mutual faithfulness and unconditional love that comes from Him to you, and this waiting "shall renew their strength; they shall mount up with wings as eagles; they shall run and not be weary; and they shall walk, and not faint" (Isa. 40:31). That is why He is your peace in your battles. When your earth starts to shake and your mountains tremble, you will not be afraid! Smyrna Christians have committed all to Him.

The unwise and the unsaved will persecute the Smyrna-type saints. Scoffing will continue in the world. They will say your message is out of time, that the old way of talking and living is out of sync. But all these things that they don't understand are biblical proof of the bride in the making. Satan and his people will accuse. Even so, he is still a loser. Jesus promised these saints in Revelation 2:10 a crown of life if they remain faithful. So don't keep your eyes on the promised wedding garment but on the Promiser, the Groom! Smyrna Christians walk by what God says and not by what they see. They hold fast to their confession knowing that what God has promised, He will fulfill! They know that He is faithful all the time. They grow to the level of knowing Jesus and the Holy Spirit as their comfort and shelter. He is a tower of refuge and strength. We can grow in our desire to praise Him not for what He promises or does but just because He is. If we are breathing, we should be praising Him.

> Let every thing that hath breath praise the
> Lord. Praise ye the Lord. (Ps. 150:6)

Give Jesus your true love. He is in love with you. We need a
den of Daniels bowing down in worship—the whole den of Daniels
kneeling before the Lord, our Maker, as His people, the holy flock
under His care. They have found intimacy with God in the secret
place and rise up to praise with a holy roar.

The Smyrna church loves to see Jesus glorified and lifted up. In
contrast, the Laodiceans need the Holy Spirit to teach His church
and stir the hearts of the people. They need to proclaim from their
hearts that they don't deserve what they ask of Him. As Jesus begins
to draw the church to Himself, it will be apparent that these are trying to retreat. But God's people cannot be drawn away if upon the
first drawing of the Lord, they will run after Him. The unwise step
or walk slowly. The wise *run* and don't walk! As you are waiting, beg
Jesus to allow you to abide in Him and He in you. Focus your longing on Him and His return. If He needs to bring you to your knees,
then allow Him to do so! Welcome this as a proof of His love for you.
Ask Jesus to take over your life. He alone has the right to take over.
That is the example He gave to Joshua.

Sometimes God will allow a test of our obedience and trust.
Keep believing and don't doubt. In Joshua 5:13–14, we read,

> And it came to pass, when Joshua was by
> Jericho, that he lifted up his eyes and looked,
> and, behold, there stood a man over against him
> with his sword drawn in his hand: and Joshua
> went unto him, and said unto him, Art thou for
> us, or for our adversaries?

Sounds like a legitimate question to ask. No one thought he'd
hear the answer that was given him in verse 14: "And he said, Nay;
but as the captain of the host of the Lord am I now come!" Let us
stop right here. He didn't say "I've come for you, Joshua," or for the

other camp. He did say who he was and that he now had come. Read on and see what the man of God did.

> And Joshua fell on his face to the earth, and
> did worship, and said unto him, What saith my
> lord unto his servant?

Read the next verse to see that this is Jesus before Bethlehem. It's not an angel because angels will never receive worship and angels never tell people to take off their shoes for they are standing on holy ground. Theologians call this an epiphany. The captain of the host is saying to Joshua, "I'm taking over!" When he takes over, He then is free to help as He knows what is best for all. Then if you stumble and fall, your captain of the host says, "I will not forsake you." He was the fourth man in the furnace, with the three Jewish teenagers. Read it in Daniel 3:25. Can we proclaim today "O, what a glorious God!"?

For the Smyrna-type Christians, their greatest love in life is Jesus. They know that their Almighty God is a Father to the fatherless. They know that He is the only One who can bring their dreams to fruition, for His glory according to His will. When they were lonely, they did find favor, and He lifted their heads and comforted them. They have read and believe and experienced Psalm 73:25–26.

> Whom have I in heaven but thee? And there
> is none upon earth that I desire beside thee. My
> flesh and my heart faileth: but God is the strength
> of my heart, and my portion forever.

That is why they declare, "I will follow You faithfully!"

7

If It Be So…

If it be so, our God whom we serve is able to deliver us from the burning fiery furnace, and He will deliver us out of thine hand, O king.
—Daniel 3:17

This quote from one of the three Hebrew teenagers (or all three collectively) is appropriate for all the Philadelphia Christians today. The King was Nebuchadnezzar, who at the time was the most powerful earthly potentate recorded. He had wanted worship and allegiance from all his citizens in all his dominions. He represents all evil systems that gain temporary earthly power from the evil one, the prince of darkness, Satan. Therefore, his evil, carnal ways represent any system—even church systems—that have lost their first love (if they ever had one) or have become lukewarm.

The heroes of faith who proclaimed a humble but heartfelt declaration are: Hananiah, Mishael, and Azariah, the close friends of Daniel, who were forced to leave Israel as a result of the conquest of their nation and were subsequently found living in Babylon. These four heroes of our faith represent the true born-again Christian surrendering all his ways to the Lordship of Jesus. Note the next thing they say in Daniel 3:18 is this: "But if not, be it known unto thee, O king, that we will not serve thy gods, nor worship the golden image which thou hast set up."

What are these false gods today? They are the same as they've always been, many of which I have already named in previous chapters and which are explained in 1 John 2:15–16 and Revelation 3:17–18. Today's false gods are being worshipped in a sophisticated manner that comes disguised as religion. Nebuchadnezzar's false gods are often called nondenominational stagnation. These are rituals brought on by pastors, hirelings that have never been called by God to the ministry.

An example of this form of false worship is practiced, to the glee of Satan, every Sunday. My wife and I visited a once mainline evangelical church in Oregon recently. Prior to attending, we phoned to ask a few questions, and we were told that they still have a midweek service and still use the King James Version of the Bible from the pulpit.

When we arrived, the doors were locked. We could see people inside, and the lights were turned on. This small-town church parking lot had eight to ten cars parked, as well as a church van, giving us the impression of some activity. We tried every door, but they were all locked. We then read a very small sign that could just barely be seen, which instructed us to "push the button" if the door was locked. We did, and a person came to open the door for us and led us to the adult prayer meeting/Bible study.

There were about 20–25 adults attending. The children were in another room. Does this sound typical? Yes, but here is the problem. The hireling took prayer requests, and the people responded as they have for probably the past fifty years: they stated their needs concerning sickness, employment, bereavement, traveling mercies, and salvations. These are typical prayer requests heard anywhere across the USA. The problem in this Laodicean church was that sickness was not approached as directed in James 5:14.

> Is any sick among you? Let him call for the
> elders of the church: and let them pray over him,
> anointing him with oil in the name of the Lord...

What about the prayer for employment? There was no mention of Jehovah-Jireh (which means "my provider") from Genesis 22:14, where God provides a ram for the burnt offering to replace Isaac on the altar. Tell me, has God changed? Does He not still have all power and might? How about bereavement? Again, the answers for Philadelphia Christians are found in the Scriptures, not in the tradition of men, which is a form of false worship. The Holy Spirit is still the Comforter. God is still Jehovah-shalom. God is peace, *our* peace.

> Then Gideon built an altar there unto the Lord, and called it Jehovah-Shalom... (Judg. 6:24)

I am not against prayer or prayer meetings. I do advocate Ephesians 6:18, "Praying always with all prayer and supplication in the Spirit, and watching thereunto with all perseverance and supplication for all saints." Note the phrase "in the Spirit." This means not in the flesh (tradition) but being led by the Holy Spirit, praying about things that are known to be in God's will, God's way, and learning to wait for God's timing.

The three Hebrew teens in the Book of Daniel, likened unto Philadelphia saints, expected a miracle. They did not demand a miracle as some hirelings indicate we should do. We cannot put any confidence in the prayer being answered if the person praying has shown himself to be unfaithful. Confidence in an unfaithful man in time of trouble is like a broken tooth, and a foot out of joint (Prov. 25:19). In times of trouble? That is when most people pray, and if someone is going to pray for us, we need him to be heard by God.

> He that turneth away his ear from hearing the law, even his prayer shall be abomination. (Prov. 28:9)

Am I against modern medicine? No! But the Laodiceans, of which that Oregon church is a typical example, have created a habit of asking for prayer requests—written or verbalized—and often the request is prayed for at that time by the pastor or another leader. Prayer is often generalized, as if presenting a shopping list for God to take care of. If the person making the request is known or active in the church family, there may be a bit of emotion behind the prayer. This style seems to be off course mostly in prayers for healing. The congregation receives the words of the prayer as non-serious communication and can be later heard expounding the merits of medical procedures or tests that they plan to seek in the future. The tone and demeanor seem to indicate that they place more value on the medical expertise than on the effectual prayer. This equals a prayer of unbelief. How can God answer the prayer? I believe one should seek verification of one's healing from a doctor and use that verification as basis for his testimony of healing, thus edifying the church.

The three who prayed at that meeting in Oregon all said practically the same thing, word for word, as if the first one had not even prayed or had not prayed correctly. Then the pastor, an interim pastor as it turned out, prayed the same prayer for the same people again. Jesus warned the hypocrites, the Pharisees, "Why do ye also transgress the commandment of God by your tradition?" (Matt. 15:3). He repeats this instruction when He quotes from Isaiah 29:13.

> Wherefore the Lord said, For as much as this people draw near me with their mouth, and with their lips do honor me, but have removed their heart far from me, and their fear toward me is taught by the precept of men: therefore, behold, I will proceed to do a marvelous work among this people, even a marvelous work and a wonder: for the wisdom of their wise men shall perish, and the understanding of their prudent men shall be hid.

And there is this from Matthew 15:

> This people draweth nigh unto me with their mouth, and honoreth me with their lips; but their heart is far from me.

The Philadelphia saints speak or pray what God's Holy Spirit has birthed in their hearts.

The heart of the wise teacheth his mouth,
and addeth learning to his lips. (Prov. 16:23)

If you don't gain victory or don't become an overcomer by continuing in the same old habits, then change your habits! Otherwise, you'll be bowing down to a false god called tradition. These Laodicean lukewarm, who perhaps never had a true first love, know nothing about *Jehovah-Nissi* (the Lord is my banner) as seen in Exodus 17:15. This banner was a flag or banner or pole-like standard beneath which the armies of God rallied. It was lifted up to call His people to battle or instruction. The altar built by Moses was built in recognition of the powerful presence, the manifested presence of *Yahweh*. Moses was honoring his God, not his tradition, as the giver of victory over their enemy, the Amalekites. The Jewish teens Shadrach, Meshach, and Abednego, knew that *Jehovah-Nissi* would give them victory over the furnace of Nebuchadnezzar!

The other problem we encountered at this Oregon Laodicean-type church was what followed the prayers. The church had locked all the unsaved people out, but the hireling gave a salvation message (very basic and with no call for repentance) to a group of already lukewarm saints. As usual, the message went in one ear and out the other. There was no altar call! There was no chance for anyone to rededicate or give their hearts or lives to the Savior. Perhaps this is somehow connected with the next thing we noticed: there was no cross inside or outside the church building.

When the meeting was over, the "pastor" came to say hello to us. He knew, of course, that we were visitors and engaged us in the expected small talk. I asked him why there was no cross in the church. He said that they used to have one behind the baptismal font but took it down. So how do you become a Philadelphian—on fire for Jesus like the three Hebrew teenagers—and still live in your Babylon? You tell Jesus in your prayer closet that you are looking for a place where you can lay your head upon His breast, the place where

He will pour His oil all over you. Ask for the oil of perfect peace. Tell Him you are looking for that refuge where you can be alone with Him. Tell Him you want to go beyond the outer courts and through the holy place, past the brazen altar, as seen in Exodus 26.

You should not be content with being among the crowds of people, the mere praisers. Saints like the three Hebrew children want to go to the holy of holies because they hunger and thirst for Christ's righteousness. They know they can only get there by the blood of the Lamb. It will take more than a casual "hurry up and get this service over with" on Sunday. They will need, as the prophet Isaiah did, the touch of the holy coal to their lips to cleanse them. These saints have learned from Ecclesiastes 12 that the conclusion, when all has been heard, is to stand in reverent awe of God and love Him enough to keep His commandments. They experience awe or fear of God as their world, their earth, shakes at the sound of His voice. They know from testimonies of true believers that Babylon does fall.

These Philadelphian saints are preparing themselves for the day of Christ's coming by asking for the fire of His love to burn within them. They want their old, hard, earthly hearts to be consumed by Him, believing that it will restore the soul. They have only one desire: to abide in His holiness. They want to be close to His side, near to His heart; and they show reverent respect by calling Him the great I AM, God Almighty, the King of Majesty! These saints desire the Lord to reign in their lives. They know that their God is a consuming fire, so His fire can protect or even consume the fire made by any false king.

> The hills melted like wax at the presence of the Lord, at the presence of the Lord of the whole earth. (Ps. 97:5)

This all begins by recognizing how beautiful our Savior is and how wonderful He will always be. The three Hebrew children knew for sure that all their days were held in His hand and engineered into His perfect plan. They prayed for God to teach them to live all of their lives not through their own eyes or the world's eyes, but through His eyes only. They have such a love for Him that they are captured—and prefer it—by His holy calling. The furnace of the false king, Nebuchadnezzar, is presented as an illustration of how our temporary inconvenience is allowed so we can learn how He is more than able to deliver. It must be, therefore, that our inconvenience is part of His great plan.

God, in His wisdom, will then administer (or allow) a test. It will come as a trial or a tribulation or some other event that has a similar feeling. It is done so we will learn that God gives us choices. Do we choose righteously or carnally or sinfully? Sometimes the test will reveal to us our own unrenewed mind and our own unchanged heart. The outcome of the test usually causes Philadelphian saints to cry out to Jesus, the Lord, to take them and mold them, to fill them with a power base different than they had before, that they may use this power in His Kingdom and allow Him to guide them. The scripture they use is Jeremiah 18:6.

> O house of Israel, cannot I do with you as
> this potter? saith the Lord. Behold, as the clay is
> in the potter's hand, so are ye in mine hand, O
> house of Israel.

This chapter tells us that God is sovereign over His people. What the potter creates depends on the nature and intrinsic qualities of the clay; what our Lord makes of His people depends on their response. We need to voluntarily give our past, present, and future to the loving hands of the Potter. Oh, to have the power and the glory of His name—the Potter—revealed to us!

Clay needs water to enable it to dry firmly. Pray for only the River of Life that brings refreshing times. It brings to the clay abundant life, which no other water can bring. The clay will then dry out and say, "I can't live without Your love or breathe without Your breath." Tell me, Saint, can anyone touch your heart like the Potter does? His mercy flows in this river. You will find not only molding but healing in these tender hands. At the same time, He will remain your defender and provider as He walks beside you every day. This will strengthen you before you get to the false king's furnace; and you too will declare His wonders and compassion and care for all, even the false king. These lessons are ways He uses to teach us how to honor Him. You won't fall; you will stand when others fall or when they cannot stand.

The three Hebrew (Philadelphia-type) saints bring their gratitude to the King of all kings! They offer, over and over, their lives in sacrifice and ministry unto their Living God. He gave you beautiful garments of praise, not for a show but to minister unto Him.

> But ye are a chosen generation, a royal priesthood, an holy nation, a peculiar people, that ye should shew forth the praises of Him who hath called you out of darkness and into His marvelous light. (1 Pet. 2:9)

8

Mostly Free or Free!

If a person, a Christian, is mostly free, then he or she is partly in bondage, tied up, ensnared, and clearly not loose. To the shame of some Christians, they don't even wish to be *free*. That is because they like their sin and are comfortable with it, at least a portion of it or for a season of it. Paul wrote this to the Church of Rome: "For all have sinned, and come short of the glory of God" (Rom. 3:23). We've already talked briefly about this verse, and most of my readers will be able to quote it.

No person will ever reach God's standard of absolute moral perfection and be worthy of His glory on his own. Remember, we are talking in kingdom-of-God terms, words, and truths here. Our source is the Bible, not our own feelings or beliefs that originate outside of the Bible. The few who understand this eternal kingdom-of-God truth are the Philadelphia-type of saints, who are not satisfied with this world or the false teachings of hirelings. They are grateful for the redemption seen in Romans 3:24. They understand via revelation truth that the redemption (the Greek word is *apolutrosis*) means "a release secured by the payment of a ransom—a deliverance and setting free of the captive."

The Smyrna- and Philadelphia-type Christians are able to persevere and gracefully bear persecutions, trials, lies, and mocking. Why? They have received the Shepherd's truth by being close to Him. He has ultimately taught them that He set them free; therefore, they are free indeed. They love God enough to say, "I want to keep Your law even though I am completely liberated from the curse of the law." Many know, however, that these people go to the next step and proclaim they wish to be servants of the Most High God! They ask for and receive Holy Spirit help for the ability instead of just the desire not to be entangled with this yoke of slavery. This starts by humbling oneself and crying out, "Help me! I need Your grace, not just for keeping me out of hell, but to save me from bondage. I want Your grace to flow like water. I need Your mercy. Please let it fall like Oregon rain."

These saints admit that they are helpless. They have learned that they need, not just desire, Him to set their lives aflame as a sacrifice. These saints plead for Holy Spirit help and want to have a burning within their hearts of His true desire. They have learned that there is so much in the world, self, and even the church that is distracting; they ask for a spiritual ear to listen when the Spirit of God speaks.

They know others need this too, so they ask for help to be bold and to be fearless to take a kingdom-of-God stand. They go to the throne of grace and plead for an anointing. Why do they ask for such an anointing? Because with the anointing, they will experience God working through them with signs and wonders. They ask Jesus to confirm His word as in the days of old. They have no rest in their spirit because of these verses:

> Verily, verily, I say unto you, He that believeth on me, the works that I do shall he do also; and greater works than these shall he do; because I go unto my Father. And whatsoever ye shall ask in my name, that will I do, that the Father may be glorified in the Son. If ye shall ask any thing in my name, I will do it. (John 14:12–14)

> Therefore I say unto you, What things soever ye desire when ye pray, believe that ye receive them, and ye shall have them." (Mark 11:24)

These saints hunger and thirst for a *rhema* from the Holy Spirit and are not just satisfied with the *logos* they respect and love so much. Obviously, one cannot have doubt, fear, little faith, underdeveloped faith, or unbelief. These saints know that to obtain these results, their requests must comply with 1 John 5:14–15.

> And this is the confidence that we have in Him, that, if we ask any thing according to His will, He heareth us: And if we know that He hear us, whatsoever we ask, we know that we have the petitions that we desired of Him.

Serious saints look at this seriously and not casually. The Word said "we know," not "we hope" or "we think, maybe." That kind of unrenewed mind will never get a saint his petition. Are these verses then only for the early believers or "super saints"? No! This verse is for the believers who have grown into Christians of the same hearts and minds as Paul and Barnabas when they ministered the Gospel at Lystra under the new power base of the Holy Spirit. Paul "said with a loud voice, Stand upright on thy feet. And he leaped and walked" (Acts 14:10). This man was crippled from his mother's womb and had never walked. Look not at the miracle but what followed the miracle in verses 11–13:

> Now when the people saw what Paul had done, they lifted up their voices, saying in the Lycaonia language, The gods have come down to us in the likeness of men!

Look particularly at verse 12:

> And Barnabas they called Jupiter; and Paul, Mercurius, because he was the chief speaker.

Stop for a minute, and allow me to add some historical facts. The Greeks worshipped Zeus and Hermes, whom the King James

Bible calls Jupiter and Mercurius. Names in different languages make no difference. In America, it could have been Elvis, Frank Sinatra, or any well-known sports figure. These two Greek gods were the father and the messenger of the gods in ancient Lystra, and the people thought this is who Paul and Barnabas were. Let's get back to Acts 14:13.

> Then the priest of Jupiter, which was before their city, brought oxen and garlands unto the gates, and would have done sacrifice with the people.

Most people in the position of Paul and Barnabas, and even many hirelings, would have taken advantage of that and accepted the praise and worship, thereby following their leader, the devil. Not Paul and Barnabas! The apostles did the opposite. They behaved more like Joseph when Potiphar's wife wanted him to lie with her, and he ran from this sinful situation—even though it caused him to be put in prison. These three saints of God (Paul, Barnabas, and Joseph) had a heart for God, His ways, and His teachings.

The question on the floor for all of us is this: how do Christians become this strong? These people set, or fix, their sights on Jesus after they have given their hearts to the only begotten Son of God. Why? Because they have learned through daily experiences that He has given them life to run the straight and narrow way. These saints try their best to please Jesus every day while knowing that every phase of their life is a test. However, they claim and stake their claim to this promise from their Savior: "Come unto me, all ye that labor and are heavy laden, and I will give you rest" (Matt. 11:28).

They receive Holy Spirit strength when they go to Him. They receive the promised Holy Spirit power. How did they receive this promised Holy Spirit power? They asked believing and not doubting! As this happens, they soon realize that the approval of men, including self, grows dim when in the presence of a holy God. They go through trials and temptations, like all of God's people; but His

MOSTLY FREE OR FREE!

presence causes the darkest fears to melt away. Why? They no longer just read Proverbs 18:24. They have experienced its truth.

> A man that hath friends must shew himself friendly: and there is a friend that sticketh closer than a brother."
> And another, "Henceforth I call you not servants; for the servant knoweth not what his Lord doeth: but I have called you friends; for all things that I have heard of my Father I have made known unto you." (John 15:15)

These saints have so much love and thankfulness for Jesus that even though He doesn't call them servants, they long to serve Him. When they come into His presence, they now know that this is where they belong, and only in His presence are their hearts and lives changed. They realize that His kingdom is established as they live to know Him more. They, having a heart change, long to follow Him. They long to know His will and have no doubts when they are in His will. They cry out, "Lord, let me live to serve Your call." While in His presence, they lift up holy hands in surrender and obedience. You can be this type of Christian. Place Jesus on the highest place and know that He is your great high priest. You can come to Him and worship at His feet.

> Now of the things which we have spoken this is the sum: We have such an high priest, who is set on the right hand of the throne of the Majesty in the heavens. (Heb. 8:1)

Saints who do this have learned by illumination truth that the work of Christ is so superior to the ministry of the Jewish Aaronic priests that by it, the old system is not needed, and God in His wisdom and mercy has replaced it with the eternal and perfect priesthood of Jesus the Christ. Even though they are allowed to come boldly to the throne of grace, they bow their knee before His throne.

As a priest who ministers to God, they offer up a song of praise. Their desire is not to please men but to bring pleasure to the love of their life. They come every day to seek the Giver, not His gifts. These saints have studied the scriptures to find out how God wants and deserves to be worshipped. They never insert human understanding or vocabulary to explain the words found in John 4:23.

> But the hour cometh, and now is, when the true worshippers shall worship the Father in spirit and in truth: for the Father seeketh such to worship Him.

Notice in this verse there is a designation between "true" and all other types of worshippers. Also notice the word *seeketh* is not past tense or present tense but is always present and future tense. The Greek word used in this verse for *true* is *aletheia*, which means "the opposite of fictitious, feigned, or false." It means sincerity, reality, accuracy, and integrity. The word *worship* used in this verse is the Greek word *proskuneo*, which comes from *pros* (toward) and *kuneo* (to kiss). It is "to prostrate oneself, bow down, and do obeisance as an act of courtesy, reverence, and adoration." It is an action, not a concept. It denotes homage rendered to God and to Christ. The Hebrew word is *shachaw*. The root word means "to depress, flatten, or to prostrate." The definition of the word is the same as the Greek definition above.

These saints have spiritually prostrated themselves even though they may have physical disabilities which inhibit the actual motion. If they were able, they certainly would prostrate themselves; but able or not, their hearts are prostrated before the loving God. They see themselves in this act and take comfort that God sees their hearts.

The fact that one has chosen to prostrate himself is evidence that he has chosen to worship. He doesn't wish to be like the lukewarm standing outside His presence and having no desire to go deeper in. These saints elevate this privileged moment instead of treating it as a common, passing thing on the way to resuming their own business. These Philadelphian believers would never keep silent and withhold from God the praise He deserves. What they have done is give their hearts to their Maker. They do not lock themselves up in lukewarmness. They discovered that at one time, they may have been lukewarm…but never again.

These saints want to love Him more each day. They want to be more willing to obey. They say, "Wow, I'm part of the royal priesthood! I wish to know the joy of sacrifice. I trust You, my faithful God, because You know what is best for me." These saints long to feast at the table of the Lord while being surrounded by His glory. They would never even sing a song that says, "I've had enough of Jesus," but only sing songs that ask for more of Him, His teachings, and His ways. Who could ever say to the Bread of Life, "I've had enough of You"? Only the lukewarm! These saints tell others, "I'll never be the same again. I can never return to the old dead way. My Lord is the door, and He shuts the old out and opens the new forever." They turn to the Lord and say, "You have the perfect plan for my life. Do it, Lord, in me!"

The Philadelphia saints, the Paul and Barnabas believers, praise their Savior every day, not just on Sunday and at midweek service. They praise Him and His name even if He does not heal them or bless them. This is a bride-to-bridegroom love affair that magnifies and glorifies their first love. They have known through life's trials that the King of kings has been with them when nobody else cared and will continue to be with them in all things. They bow down and worship with all of their hearts.

Where does this love attitude come from? Psalm 46:10. This type of lover of Jesus finds something that very few Christians ever find, which can only be found in the silence of God's majesty. There is no outside clatter of any degree, so this saint is absorbed in the new sound: the heavenly stillness of God's glory. The Hebrew word for *glory* is *kabad*. It means "weightiness that refers to copious splendor." In Greek, the word is *doxa*, which means dignity and honor. Here in this unique place and atmosphere, the true worshipper longs to hear His voice in a gentle whispering way.

The result is very humbling, and all a faithful believer wishes to do is to stand in awe before his God and willingly lay his life before Him. He might recognize the heavenly host but probably not, for they have come to worship God alone! They stand in awe but without fear because of the cleansing of the blood of Christ. They reach their hands toward the lover of their soul. He, the Mighty God, knows that they adore Him with all their heart; and He allows them to know it as well.

As this love affair grows, they recognize the power and the glory of His name and presence. They have spiritual eyes that can see the beauty that is all around them. They are overwhelmed by how the heavens stand in awe of the King. They cry out, "In Your presence, that's where I belong." They know for certain that there will not be any kind of attack, temptation, or destructive river that could overflow them. They know the reality of the three Hebrew teenagers' faith and say, "What blazing fire? I have no worry about evil or the schemes of the evil dark one, and it's all because I am in the presence of a holy God!"

None of this is possible if you are not born again or if you only know about God but don't *know* Him. It won't happen if you have never allowed Jesus to be Lord of your life and you only want Him as your Savior so that you won't go to hell. The lukewarm of Revelation 3 won't experience it. Jesus said he would spew them out. That means they won't be in; therefore, they must no longer have an intimate relationship with the Savior.

Please reread Revelation 3:15–16. The historical context of Laodicea is that of a banking and pharmaceutical center. Notice the reference Jesus makes concerning their faith being lukewarm (which He disapproves of, then and today) instead of hot or cold (which He does approve of, then and today). Jesus implies that hot and cold are equally positive. How can that be? The fact that Jesus uses both words can be explained hermeneutically and by examples in the Bible which describe intimacy with God.

He speaks to the Jews in the Old Testament and Christians in the New Testament. For example, in Psalm 23, He invites His people to times of refreshing and says He leads them to still water, where there are times of refreshing. In the New Testament, Jesus is the Living Water; and he invites His people to come and experience refreshing life, allowing it to flourish and flow to others. The hot is therapeutic; the cold is refreshing. But the lukewarm is nauseating.

Jesus deserves *absolute* devotion, and contrary to the popular belief of the hirelings, He rejects improvident (careless and rash); dilatory (tardy, time wasting, and procrastinating); and pococurante (indifferent) followers. Zeal for the Lord is not optional for those who love Him as the love of their life. Devotion willingly submits to Jesus's discipline because it recognizes His love in it.

9

A Love Worth Dying For

Paul wrote the church at Philippi and told them early in his epistle this truth: "For to me to live is Christ, and to die is gain" (Phil. 1:21). One cannot write this depth of feeling unless he has experienced an event which left a lasting impression in his soul. He had earlier stood and watched the religious people of his time lay down their clothing and/or coats at his feet as he witnessed and approved the stoning of Stephen unto death as recorded in Acts 7. He probably remembered Stephen kneeling down and crying out with a loud voice as recorded in Acts 7:59–60.

> And they stoned Stephen, calling upon God, and saying, Lord Jesus, receive my spirit. And he kneeled down, and cried with a loud voice, Lord, lay not this sin to their charge. And when he had said this, he fell asleep.

Perhaps Paul, who was known as Saul, thought about Stephen's earlier words: "Behold, I see the heavens opened, and the Son of Man standing on the right hand of God" (verse 56). Seeing and hearing this would have an impact on me; maybe not Paul, but it would have struck me! What motivates someone such as Stephen to take such a stand for Christ, a position he knew would cause such a negative reaction by those he was speaking to? Faith? Yes! Hope? Yes! Love? Yes, but not a natural love—a supernatural love. This love for

God and His ways and His teachings allows these people to lift their voices, their hands, and their lives as an offering.

They easily declare to God first, and then to all, that everything they have and are or hope to be they will give to their Maker. They know from scriptures that in heaven they will receive crowns, but they don't want them, and they will cast them before the One on the throne out of love and respect. They will cry out with the language of the angels: Holy! Holy! Holy! They don't wait to get to heaven to do this. They know that while on earth heaven can be experienced, because wherever Jesus is, that is heaven! Therefore, heaven is in their hearts.

They gather with like-minded believers to bless Him. They gather with other family members to praise Him and make hell-shaking proclamations of His faithfulness and mercy. They give Him glory and honor and are always seeking His face in celebratory gathering. They can do this because Jesus has clothed them with His righteousness and they are covered by His great love. How could they not give Him glory since God's lovingkindness has come to them?

They know God is preparing something unknown to any human on Earth. It does not bother them that they cannot comprehend it, nor do they want to, because their hearts are overflowing with gratitude as they realize that they are now His own sons and daughters. Stop and think about it! He gives all these good things freely!! They declare aloud: "Father, we will embrace Your move as the Holy Spirit prepares a Bride for Jesus." All their ugly pride is being torn down. They say "Yes, Lord" before the request is made known. They rejoice because they know that Jesus has fire in His eyes but it is from a burning desire that His bride be with Him, right next to Him! Jesus becomes their confidence even if the religious crowd is picking up stones.

These saints, like Stephen and other martyrs, look deep into His holiness and gaze into His loveliness long before anyone picks up a stone. They know from experience that all things that surround them become shadows in the light of their Savior. As their self-love diminishes, they grow deeper and deeper in love with Him; they've found the joy of reaching His heart. They have died on their cross, putting to death their will in exchange for a new will that becomes enraptured in His love. They bow down and worship the only One who is worthy. These saints want an epitaph that asks a question: Did I do my best to live for truth? Did I live my life for Jesus?

When they participated on a "worship team," did they "wing it"; or did they say, "This song is offered to a righteous God, a holy God who cannot change"? If they were teachers or pastors, did they pull their next sermon out of a computer or book, or did they receive anointing from the Holy Spirit? They ask, "Who is there like our God?" He created us in His own likeness. They declare unashamedly, "It is an honor, Lord, to worship You!"

I have been created for His pleasure, not my own. Therefore, I will press in to the heart of the Father. I will consider His grace so special that I will hold fast to it. He is a God of wonder and I will be forever grateful. The Wonderful One is truly holy and mighty. I will praise Him the way he wants to be praised. Perhaps I might lose my job or my retirement. Still, I will praise Yahweh. I will rejoice, not in the negative things, but I will rejoice in the Lord, who is my only God, my Strength, and the One I sing to and about. David said this in Psalm 34:1, "I *will* bless the Lord at all times: his praise shall continually be in my mouth." But we must do it God's way, not our way.

The Philadelphian saint looks at death in the flesh as the beginning of the second phase of eternal life. Phase one begins at the new birth from the seed of God. Then the saint dies and experiences the taking off of his corrupted "tent" (phase two). While he is alive in phase one, the hope of phase two and the fulfillment of all God's promises to him causes him to sing out, "You, Jesus, are my everything. You are my all in all." The temporary life, as well as the eternal life, receives its blessings through and because of Him, their righteousness; so they are forever seeking His face. Their desire is to live much closer and to learn from the only One who is omniscient.

Hell and destruction are before the Lord;
how much more then the hearts of the children
of men?" (Prov. 15:11)

> Great is our Lord, and of great power: His understanding is infinite. (Ps. 147:5)

> Remember the former things of old: for I am God, and there is none else; I am God, and there is none like me, declaring the end from the beginning, and from ancient times the things that are not yet done, saying, my counsel shall stand, and I will do all my pleasure. (Isa. 46:9–10)

That is why the true Philadelphia-type Christian desires to learn of God and learn from God. He cheers when the strong voice of heaven says, "See now what I can do in you." In response he cries out, "Lord, I am fascinated by Your wisdom and captivated by all that there is about You! Because You have allowed me to be consecrated to be holy and You count me in as part of the remnant, I will always be seeking You and always be declaring, 'You alone are worthy!'" These saints go through the flood or fire because Jesus gave them a love that has caused their hearts to overflow even to the unlovable. They praise their God for separating them from the world and removing their sin as far as the East is from the West.

They now have the ability to see better days ahead. No longer do they envy or emulate people of past or present notoriety who are lost for all eternity. No matter what such people may have accomplished on earth, the fact that they are lost voids any recognition by the saints because the Philadelphian is only interested in hearing Jesus say, "Well, done, thou good and faithful servant." He does not fear the words, "Depart from me, you who work iniquity."

These saints know that Jesus is the Good Shepherd who makes them lie down in green pastures. He is not a hireling. They have tasted and their hunger has been satisfied over and over again with the honey from His Word. This is because they made Jesus the Lord of everything. Those who don't make Him the Lord of everything will never gain all these benefits. All they taste is misery on earth, waiting for death so they can go to heaven.

The Philadelphia saints have the enjoyment of touching heaven and changing their world and sphere of influence. The fear that goes with doubting God's love is gone. They know that He doesn't like some of the things they do, but they are secure knowing He still loves them. This is the foremost element of God: He is eternal and unchangeable. His love remains in their hearts even if they backslide until the Holy Spirit convicts them and they repent. They cry with heavenly sorrow knowing that He holds them in His hand and that this is where they belong. They have faith to cling to His promise that He will never let them go, even when they have no thought for Him at all.

These saints take communion as an act of honor and remembrance of *every single aspect* of all the things they know of Jesus, not just that He was the Lamb that was slain for them. They rejoice when they hear His name spoken. They give praises to God for the times they found new strength when they were very weak. The enemy of their soul must leave at the name of Jesus. They dance and sing about their Redeemer, Healer, and Friend who is the Lord Almighty! They know Him as Savior and Defender and have willingly made Him the only King of their lives. These saints cannot stop telling of His loving Kindness that keeps changing their hearts from glory to glory. They tell Him and everyone else that His love is superior to anything this temporary life can offer. Their experiences prove that all they need will be found in Jesus, the Lord of Glory! Soon they sing out, "Hallelujah!"

How do you gain this love worth dying for and why don't the lukewarm have it? They don't make Jesus their Lord, nor their King. They only want to be in His Kingdom, sometime later. They sing, "I surrender all," but only as a classic church hymn and not as the truth of their lives. The problem is that they run into three spiritual detours on the way to kingdom life: rebellion (I won't), resentment (why do these things happen to me?), and dependence on self (I'd rather do it myself). How do you overcome these hindrances? The answer is found in Hebrews 5:8.

> Though He were a Son, yet learned He obedience by the things which He suffered.

You and I can't overcome these on our own. God must do it for us. He purges us from the inside, deep in our hearts. This is seen in the illustration told in John 15:1–2.

> I AM the true vine, and my Father is the husbandman. Every branch in me that beareth not fruit He taketh away: and every branch that beareth fruit, He purgeth it, that it may bring forth more fruit.

In order to be productive, we, the branches, must submit to pruning and then maintain an abiding love affair with the true vine.

Another reason most Christians never grow to a higher spiritual level is because of what I will call alignment. The alignment has to do with the will of God. The English word *will* comes from two Greek words which define two types of will. The first is *boulema*. It refers to the eternal counsels of God and will be done regardless of how we feel about it. For example, it is God's *boulema* (God's will) that when we fall, we fall down instead of up. He created us, and this is how he designed gravity and no amount of disagreement on our part will make us fall in any other direction. God's *boulema* (God's will) is seen in the eternal plans He has set in motion.

The second word for will, *thelema*, is His sincere desire for all His creation (Matt. 6:10, 8:2, 12:55). But the fulfillment of God's desire can be hindered by events in the creation (John 6:39). For example, it is God's will and desire (*thelema*) that all be saved (2 Peter 3:9) but we know that all are not willing or desirous of being saved. Because they will not align themselves with His will they will not be saved. We can align ourselves with God by agreeing with His will. His *boulema* will occur as he planned.

God's will sets the standard we live by. The "will of the church" should not set a standard for us. The pastor's will should not set a standard for us. All actions will be measured against God's standard and no other (John 8:29). Jesus said, "And He that sent Me is with Me: the Father hath not left Me alone; for I do always those things that please Him."

As a new believer you may find it difficult to line up with His will in spite of your desire to do so. As your heart is changed, the difficulty decreases and the ability increases. You prove to yourself that you are a continuer, continuing on the straight and narrow. This tells us that Jesus's will and the Father's will were and are one and the same. How does this happen? Although Jesus knew God's will as Son of God, when He was born in Bethlehem He had to learn to know and do God's will as the Son of man, including coping with trials and tribulations of such extremes as being tempted by Satan, mocked and ridiculed by His enemies, and finally crucified. The question now is: where does your will fit in? Do you have a desire to do His will or yours?

When you line yourself up with His will, you have the victory. You are on the path Jesus has called you to. This results in more victories than defeats in spiritual warfare. God, the chief husbandman, is committed to pruning you in order to develop your new nature. The new nature ensures that you will produce fruit of the Spirit. He offers you a new base—that of the empowering Holy Spirit. Peter didn't have the new ability when he denied Christ. However, after Pentecost, he did have a new base with power to do God's will. Jesus said this: "If ye then, being evil, know how to give good gifts unto your children: how much more shall your heavenly Father give the Holy Spirit to them that ask Him?" (Luke 11:13).

Have you asked Him? Ask now for the blessing of the Holy Spirit. Ask in faith, and you will receive and have a new base operating in your life.

10
Time to Make a Choice

I have written about four types of churches in the church age, from Pentecost to the present time. Even though Jesus addresses other churches in their respective eras, these four best represent current church policy. Two are positive, and two are negative. The Smyrna and Philadelphia churches are role model churches. The main difference between the two "wise" churches and the two "unwise" and foolish churches has to do with their understanding and acceptance of the Lordship of Jesus Christ. You, and all Christians, have to make a choice.

The churches at Smyrna and Philadelphia accepted Jesus as Savior much like the other two. However, the two wise churches followed Jesus while the unwise only tagged along after Him. The church at Smyrna followed faithfully. What is the difference? Judas tagged along after Jesus. The scribes tagged along after Jesus. Peter, James, and John followed Jesus. The Smyrna and Philadelphia Christians don't tag along behind. They are purposeful followers as described in 1 Corinthians 11:1, "Be ye followers [*mimos*] of me, even as I also am of Christ."

Usually Bible words translated *follow* (followed or following) are written with a different word which means "tag along"; but this verse specifically uses the Greek word *mimos*, which means "to be traced upon." It is the origin of our English word *mimic*. It means that you are the paper, and you allow Jesus to be the stencil. It means you want to conform to Him in all ways; so you plead for Him to trace Himself and His character onto your heart, soul, and mind. This type of following results in demonstrative manifestations as promised by Jesus in Mark 16:7–18.

Perhaps the Holy Spirit has touched your heart with the desire to leave the theoretical behind, and seek the "traced-upon" life that is characterized by experiencing the promises of Mark 16 and the Book of Acts. Jesus also promised the Philadelphia Christians that they would not have to face the wrath to come. Thinking on this will usually make a person more evangelical in that they do not want people to go to hell after death. That is an honorable thought, and all Christians should want to please Christ regarding what many call the Great Commission found in Matthew 28:18–20.

> And Jesus came and spake unto them, All power is given unto Me in heaven and in earth. Go ye therefore, and teach all nations, baptizing them in the name of the Father, and of the Son, and of the Holy Ghost: Teaching them to observe all things whatsoever I have commanded you: and lo, I am with you alway, even unto the end of the world. Amen.

However, my focus has not been a treatise for evangelism but a treatise for God who deserves a holy lifestyle from His children. Unfortunately, the hirelings have not taught or encouraged a holy lifestyle. I base this on two biblical truths which have been stolen by the antichrist-age false teachers. First, 1 John 3:2 says, "Beloved, now are we the sons of God, and it doth not yet appear what we shall be: but we know that when He shall appear, we shall be like Him; for we shall see Him as He is." Most hirelings who have Laodicean and/or Ephesus Christians in their congregations don't add the next verse; they act as if it is not needed. If it isn't needed, then why did the Holy Spirit give it to John to write down for all future generations to read?

> And every man that hath this hope in Him purifieth himself, even as He is pure.

Pure in Greek is *hagnos*. It comes from the same root as *hagios*—"holy." The adjective describes a person or thing that is clean and modest, pure, and undefiled, morally faultless and without blemish. "Look, Hon. Look what they've done to His church." Jesus demonstrated His zeal over the house of prayer when He saw what the people were doing at the temple.

> And Jesus went into the temple of God, and cast out all them that sold and bought in the temple, and overthrew the tables of the moneychangers, and the seats of them that sold doves, and said unto them, "It is written, My house shall be called the house of prayer; but ye have made it a den of thieves. (Matt. 21:12–13)

The hirelings today must believe that Christ would just "wink" at the food and drink dispensed freely or sold in the churches and then brought into the sanctuary. And what about the rummage sales held in the actual sanctuary of the church? "Look what they've done to His church, Hon." No, I'm not being legalistic; I'm being Bible-istic.

The second truth for writing this book is similar to the one we read in 1 John 3:2, the verse which should motivate Christians to live righteously. Now we look at Revelation 19:7.

> Let us be glad and rejoice, and give honor to Him: for the marriage of the Lamb is come, and His wife hath made herself ready.

It's hard to make yourself ready if you've lost your fist love. It's hard to make yourself ready if some liar says to you, "You are ready. Jesus loves you just as you are." Yes, He does love us and always has. But do you love Him? Take a lesson from scripture; consider why the five wise were taken in and the five unwise were not taken in even after their late and pathetic pleading. The correlation is found in Esther 2.

The king, King Ahasuerus, wanted a wife to replace Queen Vashti. The method of selection is recorded in verse 4: "And let the maiden which pleaseth the king be queen instead of Vashti." Persian law required that the women who might have a chance to be queen observe twelve months of preparation before the selection. The question that must be asked is "How serious are you about being chosen?" How intense is your desire for the King to choose you? Are you going to be proud and say, "He'll like me just the way I am"? Or will you do as Esther did in verse 15?

> Now when the turn of Esther, the daughter of Abihail the uncle of Mordecai, who had taken her for his daughter, was come to go in unto the king, she required nothing but what Hegai, the King's chamberlain, the keeper of the women, appointed. And Esther obtained favor in the sight of all them that looked upon her.

All the young beauties of the land had access to the ointments, clothing, and perfumes. However, Esther knew that only the one who is close to the king, like a eunuch, would know what pleases the king the most!

So what is the job of the five wise? It is to find out what pleases the King of kings as His wedding approaches. Who are the eunuchs now? They are the laws of Moses, the writings of the Psalms, the prophets, the Gospels, and the Epistles of the apostles. You'll find a good description of the bride and the Bridegroom in Psalm 45. Read it and meditate on it many times. You will soon realize that you want nothing to do with a Laodicean or Ephesus kind of church as seen in all of the fifty states of America! You will do everything you need to do to become a Smyrna or Philadelphia Christian living in a Laodicean age.

Don't buy into the false teaching that you don't have to change in order to be present in the rapture. Don't believe the lie of the devil or your flesh that tells you that you can come to the King of glory for a marriage feast "just as you are." You come for salvation just as you are, but future rewards and crowns are dependent on your actual growth. An unsanctified person, looking and thinking and sounding like they did before they were called by Christ out of darkness, cannot expect the same rewards.

If it were true that we can be raptured and receive crowns at the feet of Jesus "just the way we are," then why did we need to be born again? Why did Jesus say to repent? If God the Father wishes us to stay "as you are", then why did He give the world a Savior? Why did the Holy Spirit instruct David to write Psalm 1 or Solomon to write Proverbs 1:10–15? Of course, as always, it is your choice. You have to decide. I have made my choice.

> And if it seem evil unto you to serve the Lord, choose you this day whom ye will serve; whether the gods which your fathers served that were on the other side of the flood, or the gods of the Amorites in whose land ye dwell: but as for me and my house, we will serve the Lord. (Josh. 24:15)

And now for some final counsel regarding your future: seek like-minded believers who know the value of becoming a Daniel and have learned how God deserves to be praised. The praise arising to God from His holy priesthood should not be loud just for the sake of being loud. The praise of God from His holy saints should be the sound of a holy roar ascending as a sweet sound and pleasing to God.

This causes two things to happen: 1) the omnipresence of God will become the *manifest* presence of God as He inhabits those praises, and we know that in the Bible and in church history, when this happens, there are signs, wonders, and miracles accompanying God's manifested presence; and 2) the holy roar worship causes the principalities and powers of the air and all demonic forces to *tremble*! When Jesus confronted demons, they said, "Have you come to torment us?" Hell is terrified at the presence of the King of glory. Instead of asking to be sent into a herd of swine, they will flee with terror because they know the truth of Romans 16:19–20.

For your obedience is come abroad unto all men. I am glad therefore on your behalf: but yet I would have you wise unto that which is good, and simple concerning evil. And the God of peace shall bruise Satan under your feet shortly. The grace of our Lord Jesus Christ be with you. Amen!

About the Author

S. C. Cundiff was born on July 16, 1949, in Bremerton, Washington. He, along with his wife, Georgann, was converted under the ministry of Campus Crusade for Christ and David Wilkerson during their college years. He studied Christian Education at the University of Puget Sound, graduating with a bachelor's degree in 1974. He then studied theology at Berean School of the Bible to complete his pastoral studies. From 1971 to 1993, he conducted evangelistic speaking engagements and Bible teaching ministry in the state of Washington while leading worship at the Full Gospel Businessmen's Fellowship in Bremerton.

In 2005, Steven founded LivingStones Fellowship in Lewiston, Idaho. He spoke on Liberty Christian Television and wrote articles for the local newspaper. While living and ministering there, he wrote his first book, *Wooden Nickels and Yankee Dimes* (copyright 2014). Steven and his wife had three sons, two of whom are deceased and waiting in glory, while their middle son lives with his wife and their son in Oregon. He is currently Senior Pastor of Bethel Community Church, in Bethel, Oregon.